The Angel Whispered

JEAN HALLAM

Ordering Information:

Prime Seven Media
518 Landmann St.
Tomah City, WI 54660

Printed in the United States of America

Table of Contents

IN MEMORY OF MY BEAUTIFUL
DAUGHTER KATHRYN DANIELLE

AN ANGEL IN OUR MIDSTS 1985-2011

The Angel Whispered

With love
Thank you to my Angels and all the Angels
here on this earth for your assistance

Jean Hallam

The Beginning

My life began in May 1960 in a small pretty mining village called Conisbrough in the county of South Yorkshire.

The house we lived in was a very small mid terraced house with a bright blue door and a white step that my mother used to kneel and clean it until it shone the house had the view of Conisbrough Castle.

My mum was a petite lady who always looked after herself and tried to look smart even when she was cleaning and my father was a tall thin man but broad and had very dark curly hair he wore glasses that were thick rimmed and black edged, He always enjoyed a few pints and a good laugh with his mates.

I was told it was a very hot spring sunny day when my mum went into labour with me; my father was not even around at the time probably he was at work or at the pub therefore my mother took herself to the Rose Hospital in Doncaster where she gave birth to me at 11.55 pm on a Sunday evening. I was told that my mother did not have an easy birth with me and was very weak afterwards.

When mum brought me home a week later, my father was waiting at the door with his hands outstretched he took me off her and told her to put the kettle on she brought her own bag in and my father sat with me on the settee and mum carried on as if she had not given birth to me after all she had the house hold chores to do.

I was the first born to my parents who had been trying to have a child for a long time, until I came along the marriage had been on a roller coaster, up and down so they thought that when I arrived the marriage would be saved and become better.

My mother had fostered many children and my father was a miner but my mother and father were down to earth people from very plain backgrounds but with very high morals.

So my life began …

My parents had very little money as my father always found an excuse not to go to work, he used to drink a lot quite heavily so my mum had to juggle very little money around work, household bills and look after me, also the other children that she fostered too but there was one thing the house was always spick and span that smelled of lilacs and polish.

My family were not very religious, my father used to say "these Priests and Vicars should do a proper mans job and not tell us how to live our lives!" so religion, politics and money were three forbidden subjects around the dinner table. I always knew I was different from the other children even from an early age as I used to play quite happily on my own,

(So my mother used to tell me), but I knew I was not alone I had a friend, her name was Mary and she used to be with me all the time.

She used to sit on my bed and she always wanted to play and talk to me, even when I didn't "see" her I always knew she was with me.

My earliest memory of Mary was on a cold winter morning, I heard my mum crying in the kitchen not really understanding why. As I was only small at the time, and I remember lying down on the settee which was faded red brocade and it felt very scratchy and rough on my skin.

I was looking around the room at the range with the kettle steaming on it which was charred black and the hearth was blackened and shiny where my mum had polished It to make it look like a mirror, my eyes gazed up to the window seeing how high and narrow it was, which seemed to go on forever, the reflection of the cold sun was streaming through and reflecting on the rug and hearth. Mum had net curtains at half the window and it was steaming up because of the warmth of the house. I noticed in front of the hearth on the rug my mum had made out of different coloured rags there was a tabby cat that had a bald patch on his hind leg,

He was cleaning himself in front of the fire quite contented. He was a stray that my mum used to feed occasionally. a kind looking man came in, he was a tall thin man with a grey coloured suit with grey receding hair he also had round-rimmed glasses on, he had a soft velvety voice and a gentle kind smile, in his hand was a black weathered looking bag, he felt my head and started to talk to my mother. She was wringing her hands and had a worried look on her face. He got out of his bag a stethoscope and put it on my chest and was listening with a worried look on his face,

He came back later to see me and his tone to my mum had changed, he had told my mum that he wanted to see my father at the surgery, my mum told me that my father was down at the pub that day, it had been pay day and she had no money to get the medicine for me, as she was waiting for him to come home.

The kind man who was a doctor had come back to see if I had improved with the medicine, he took the prescription from my mother and paid for the medicine himself I had contracted a respiratory tract infection.

When he came back he gave me the medicine and said to my mother to tell my father that he wanted to see him at the surgery the next morning.

When my father came home my mother told him and he just shouted at my mother and slapped her face that was the first time I witnessed my mother getting hit by my father I remember crying and my father came to pick me up which I cried louder and my mother saying to him "leave her you have frightened her" he then hugged me and tried to comfort me.

My father never went to see the doctor the next day.

Mary sat with me on the settee; I noticed she had dark curly hair that fell in ringlets. This seemed to shine like a halo round her little face. Her eyes were of the palest blue she had a little rose bud mouth that was always smiling

I was not afraid of her I thought she was a friend who came to play with me. She said "you will be alright Jeanie."

My father had hit my mother again a few weeks later for letting the electric man in to read the meter apparently my mother had previously left my father because the electric had been cut off and the Bailiffs had been and took some of my mum's belongings as payment.

Mum said she wouldn't go back to my father until he had sorted the electric out and paid the bill. He then promised my mother he would pay the bill and get it back on but unbeknown to my mother, my father had rewired the electric himself to the main electric wires outside the house so in fact we were getting the electric for free.

When he went to sort it out he told the electric company a lie, he said that I had been very sick and He had no choice but to do what he had done apparently he was so convincing that they believed him and did not charge him he was that good they even offered him a job!

This was the last straw for my mum … Of course I then went down with an illness.

Mum picked me up and had packed a bag and then she wrapped me in a blanket that had little blue and pink squares all over, it felt very soft and warm round my body we then proceeded to set off to go back to my Aunt Freda's house.

I remember my mum often had tears in her eyes and she used to hug me so tight and whisper to me "I will make sure you have a better life than this Jeanie".

Mum left me at my Aunt Freda and Uncle Joe's and then went back to see my father. While I was at my aunts house I was playing in her yard which was lower down to the house next door, as the houses travelled up in tiers I was watching the little boy on the wall above me he had some sand in a bucket then it slipped and fell onto my face covering me.

My eyes started to sting and I screamed, Uncle Joe came rushing out with my mother who had just come back from seeing my dad, Aunt Freda and uncle Joe scooped me up in their arms put my head under the tap in the enamel sink and started to wash my face the next minute I was being rushed to hospital, the sand was building sand and it had lime in it, which could have blinded me.

It was burning my eyes and my throat, they cleaned my throat out and I had have my eyes cleaned out so they froze them and popped them out onto my cheeks, cleaned them and put them back! When I was growing up I used to panic if I saw anyone throwing sand about on the beach, To this day I can't stand anyone throwing sand but Mary was there again and she kept saying "you will be all right I promise". While all this was going on I could hear my mother crying this made me feel uneasy and frightened there always seemed to have voices raised shouting, screaming and things being thrown against the walls in those days.

My mother had answered a job for a live in housekeeper in Sheffield. Little did I know at the time she had been secretly planning to leave my father for good.

Mum was very upset at going not because of my father, but because she had to send the child she was looking after back to the children's home.

My mum had got the job; the man my mum worked for was called Clive Gardner Stephenson. I noticed that he was a short dark haired man with a round tummy and had the softest brown kind looking eyes. He had a dark suit with a white shirt and a stripy tie and his shoes were very shiny!

He was sat behind a big wooden desk with lots of papers on it. I could smell polish and when I put my hands on the desk it felt very smooth and slippy under my touch.

A couple of days later my mum left my father for good and we fled to Sheffield.

When my mother divorced from my father, Mary was around me a lot during those dark times. But at least there was no shouting and my body stopped shaking.

As I settled down into a new life the days seemed to pass by very quickly, eventually my mother fell in love and married her boss Clive.

Mary told me that this man was a good man and she wasn't wrong he was, he loved me as if I was his own child in fact he adopted me as his own daughter, as my own father didn't even bother or want to see me I then started calling him daddy Clive.

Another chapter began with my new baby brother! My mum and daddy Clive decided to call my new brother Clive. This pleased my dad's mum and Alan who was my dad's older son. When mum introduced me to my brother I noticed his fat chubby feet and hands and he had a soft baby powder smell that permeated round the house.

These were happy days of my child hood and Mary still came to be with me.

When my brother was ready to go to school it was one of my jobs to take and bring him back to school with me. He started to get cheeky as he grew up and show off at times and we would end up squabbling and I always said "I am going to tell my daddy on you!" he then would say "sorry" and make me promise not to . . . sometimes I ignored him and still told mum.

But she used to ignore me and say I was telling fibs, as Clive was a good boy! I soon found out that mum was fonder of my brother than me.

Then Mary used to come to me when I was sad and in my ear she whispered "don't worry you have me and you will be ok".

To this day my mum finds something to criticise about me. She always relished saying "OH you are so much like your father a bloody pain!" this used to really hurt me as a child.

It brought resentment in me towards my brother at those times. I often felt lonely when mum was like that to me.

To the best of my knowledge I had never been to a church or inside one, so one Sunday my mother had got me dressed up in my very best clothes and my shiny shoes and told me we were to go to church with daddy Clive this was to be a turning point and the rules of life seemed to have changed.

As I entered the church I noticed the smell and the ambiance of the church the high ceilings and the greyness of the stone the pews were highly polished and they seemed to lean back as if they too were looking up to the ornate pained windows I couldn't take my eyes off the angels they seemed to look at me and connect with me I was memorised!

It was during a family get together that my gift was first noticed by certain members of the family. Mary told me that my aunty was having a baby so I went over and told my aunty that she was having a baby; she didn't know she was pregnant at the time and she just laughed it off, my mum used to say "Jeanie lives in her own imaginary world at times"!

But later on my aunt did find out she was pregnant this caused great excitement and also everyone couldn't believe that I had predicted something like that at such an early age.

My Nana said to my mum "I told you that our Jeanie has the same gift as us" so I started to ask questions what gift had I got and why? So when we visited my Nana she tried to explain and said that her own mother and her mother had the gift of premonition and she also had the same but also my own mother had the gift of premonition too.

Mum said to my nana that I was too young and that they should protect me. I was listening to all this and thought to myself "why did they have to protect me?

From what? What was premonition"? And "why couldn't I see this gift"? But when I asked, mum used to say "you will learn when you are ready but not now."

I used to watch my Nana in awe when she read the tea leaves for my mum and other people who used to visit, she would make a cup of tea and they had to drink it then she would turn the tea cup over and put it on its saucer and turn it three times she would say something that I couldn't understand but she then told them what she could "see" sometimes she would tell them without the tea leaves just by holding their hands!

As I grew older Mary seemed to disappear but I had visions and could hear voices like a whisper in my ears they came more often as I got older, I used to think I was imagining it at times! I wasn't afraid it just used to annoy me as they seemed to whisper to me non stop!

The one vivid memory I had was at the age of 10 and it has remained with me ever since, I was with my mother and dad, we were looking at houses that were for sale as we were moving from the North to the South of England.

We had looked at quite a few houses but one particular house stood out from the rest it seemed nice from the outside. It had been painted White with a nice wooden door there were flowers around the front and growing around the sides of the white gravel path the house looked very quaint from the outside.

As we entered the house both my mother and I felt uneasy and mum remarked that it was unusually cold. I on the other hand felt sick and very cold but it was a warm summer's day then I heard a scream and my eyes were drawn to the bottom of the stairs. I started to shake from head to foot my heart seemed to be jumping and beating so loudly that I thought it would jump out of me, it was then that I saw a lady on the floor in a heap,

I remember shaking my mothers arm trying to pull mum away from the stairs I just wanted to get out of the house mum asked me what I had seen as she had felt it too, through my tears I told her that it was a sad place and something bad had happened there.

It turned out after my mum and dad asked questions that the owner's wife had died in "suspicious" Circumstances she had "fallen" down the stairs and the husband had killed himself so the family wanted a quick sale needless to say mum and dad did not buy the house!

After that experience I tried to dismiss my sixth sense and ignore it, even throughout my school days I tried to ignore it I became afraid of it and I must admit I even went through a stage of blaming mum and my grandmother for giving me this unwanted gift at the time.

When I was thirteen my psychic experience came into the fore again, my father had been ill for quite some time but he was a proud man and used to say "don't worry about me stop fussing"! But it was on a cold January Sunday morning that I had an uneasy feeling all day my father was doing his Sunday chores, cleaning the car ect.

I had my usual horse-riding lesson with Margaret our neighbour, (she used to own the stables) and it was on the way home I had a vision that would be in my mind forever to this day.

It seems like only yesterday I heard a voice telling me not to let my father go in the car, then I had a vision of him slumped over the wheel, when I got home I told mum not to let dad leave the house at all, but all she said was "I know Jeanie", in a rather quiet voice. The sickness and apprehension wouldn't leave me A few hours later the night started to creep in and the temperature had dropped even more, frost was starting to show on the grass in the garden and there was a definite nip in the air,

I started to relax a little as we were just snuggling around the fire to watch the local news on the TV all of a sudden there came a rapid knock to the door,

It was Margaret our neighbour she was in tears and in a terrible state she had taken her dog for a walk near the stables and something had spooked the dog and it had bolted so she couldn't find him.

The dog was only a puppy and she hadn't had him long so my dad being the gallant man that he was said "don't worry I shall have a look for him" Margaret had told him where she had last been so off he went in the car ... Mum said to my dad not to be too long and that the police should be informed if they couldn't find him but he told mum not to worry.

I wanted to go with dad but he wouldn't hear of it and said to me "you stay here in the warmth I wont be long" patting my head and stroking my hair as he passed. A few hours later there was still no sign of dad or the dog and in those days there were no such things as mobile phones so he couldn't get in touch or vice versa for that matter.

We all started to worry and again I had the vision I felt sick to the core by this time I was drawn to the window and I kept looking out for the familiar headlights of the car willing it come up the street, but there was nothing in sight all I could see was the frost starting to glisten on the pavement like little stars twinkling and the street lamps reflecting on the deserted road.

Margaret said she would go and help my dad I said I would go with Margaret back to the area to see if we could see dad and the dog. We arrived about 15 mins later and I saw the car in the distance, the engine was running also the lights on the car were on... it was then I saw my father slumped over the steering wheel.

My heart seemed to sink rapidly and come back up and I felt sick, my mind was in overdrive because I knew deep down that I had predicted and seen it and no one had listened to me as usual.

The next few minutes seemed like hours everything just seemed to go in slow motion, but my instincts kicked in.

Margaret just looked and seemed rooted to the spot so I screamed at her to get help and pushed her which seemed to do the trick then she ran into the road to flag someone down luckily she flagged a couple and one was a doctor the other person then drove off to find the nearest telephone box.

I now know the angels sent this couple. The doctor then wrapped a blanket round my dad and was trying to talk to him.

My dad's lips were blue and his eyes kept rolling up into his head he seemed to be gasping for air as he was trying to talk to me.

I held on to my father and he whispered and gasped to me "I am sorry Jeanie". That was the last thing he ever said to me I then felt another presence that was with us as I looked the vision came from nowhere but seemed to illuminate around my dad it was then I knew the angel had come for him.

I asked even begged the angel "please, please do not to take him"! but the angel said "it is his time" the doctor looked at me as if I was going mad as he thought I was talking to him, then my dad died in my arms I felt his soul rise That was one of the darkest days I encountered. I felt so alone and lost, even Mary had deserted me.

Later when my mum had arrived back from the hospital both my little brother and I was told officially that dad had gone to heaven and then we were ushered to bed.

As I laid there exhausted from the events I could hear the muffled sounds of my mother and neighbours' talking in the lounge below me, I started to drift off to sleep I was half asleep and half awake when my dad came to me I felt his hand on my head and he stroked my hair then a voice in my ear said "I will always be here watching you" I then fell asleep, with my tears soaking the pillow.

After my Dad died my Mum wanted to go home back to Yorkshire to be near all the family she didn't want to stay in the south she said she needed to be near the family so we had no choice but to leave our beloved home and friends we had made. These were sombre days for us sadness seemed to permeate around us like a thick veil.

My mother soon settled again and started going out with her friends and had a few men friends that used to call on her, even though both my brother and I still mourned dad and missed our home and friends we were trying very hard to still "fit in" then one day out of the blue she told my brother and I that she wasn't destined to be alone and promptly introduced us to husband number three!

My brother and I, even the rest of the family were taken aback as dad had only previously died nine months ago.

This new man was twenty-one years younger than my mum; she hadn't known him for very long she only had known him about three months! Apparently she had met him at a club that she used to frequent, she used to laugh at what her nickname was she was known as "the merry widow" I was so ashamed and embarrassed of her but she seemed oblivious to the label she was attracting.

As soon as I had met this man I had a terrible feeling of doom and again I had a vision, this man was evil and I saw my mum crying. All I could see was a darkness that emanated around him the sickness and apprehension came flooding back and mild panic seemed to settle in my stomach.

Even my Nanan tried telling my mum that it wasn't right and that she would be making a big mistake and to think about Clive and me but mum wouldn't listen to her. All we got was from Mum "it's my life and I am not going to be alone and the children need a father"!

I even tried telling her of my vision but mum again said, "That I was just being "difficult" and what did I know I was only fourteen! So the wedding went ahead and the very next day . . .

My mum was punched and kicked and was told by him that he would bleed her dry. He had my mother by the throat and said in gritted teeth with his face screwed up in anger and full of hatred that he would make sure her little bastards wouldn't get a penny! Then he pushed my mother to the ground and promptly walked out mum was left gasping, crying and rubbing her bruises both Clive and I were witness to this spectacle. I was starting to get the familiar shakes and I could sense Clive was feeling the same.

My father had left us "quite "comfortable financially and we had money to live on but I knew that this was not what he would have wanted for us, I prayed and prayed that the nightmare would end.

This new man did not want me or my brother around and made our lives a misery we spent many a day even a night in our rooms just to keep out of his way.

But mum was still oblivious to our unhappiness, the house was always filled with anger and I would often retreat to my room just to get away. I felt so alone and my tears used to come so easily.

He was verbally and sometimes physically abusive to me and my brother but always when mum wasn't around us so she never heard him and never saw him, but she wouldn't have believed us anyway as she still had the rose coloured glasses on even though he was cruel to her too!

Even the family started to dissipate and we saw them less and less this was because he used to make them feel uncomfortable so we invariably went to visit them instead but even then this started to wane as when we arrived home it was always back to arguments so in the end just for a quiet life that stopped I missed seeing my Nanan and Granddad and my aunties and uncles.

As time progressed I often had a slap even the occasional punch and he threatened me on many occasion to kill me I was very afraid but I wouldn't show it to him, my strength seemed to come from somewhere, my father was with me a lot in those dark days, even Mary came back to me, but through gritted teeth and determination I vowed he would never get the better of me and one day just one day I will have the upper hand.

So the years went by and I was determined to protect my brother and myself as much as I could.

I was the usual rebellious teenager going out to parties, I was often moody but I studied hard as I was always put down by the "evil" man, he often used to say with a seethe in his voice,

"I can see it now you will end up on the dole or get yourself pregnant and just be a scrounger and you will not be living here scrounging off your mum and me"! the looks I used to get were evil I saw a darkness around him and the evil that seemed to come from his very soul which tried to bore into me I raised my head up and put my chin in the air and glared back like a mirror reflecting back the distaste I had for him too

Inside I was trembling but on the outside I was like a mighty warrior going into battle!

He would often swear at me and call me a slut deep down I knew I would prove him wrong oh yes I would certainly do that!

Like I said I was the rebellious teenager and I announced to my mum that I wanted a motorbike so I saved and saved up hard to get my new bike and I loved it, it was my freedom I could get away from the darkness that I lived in.

I loved the colour, it was lime green with black and white stripes it was a Kawasaki 750 I even had the matching helmet and leathers I used to feel good and confident on it and I also used to get around the city with so much ease.

But mum said every time I went on it "I don't like you going on it Jeanie I know you will get hurt" as daughter like mother I didn't or wouldn't listen to her. Why should I have done? as my respect for my mum had gone by then she didn't care about me only her own happiness.

When I reached twenty-one I had a huge encounter that changed my whole persona and outlook on life.

Now like I said my mother had premonitions too and I was still a little rebellious and like any young woman I had my fair share of parties and boyfriends and hadn't a care in the world I just lived life on the edge if you like enjoying myself!

It was the year of my 21st birthday and I was about to go out on my bike when a voice in my head said "don't go on it today" but I wouldn't listen to it and shook it off.

As I was getting my helmet and gloves my mum came up to me wringing her hands in despair she stopped me in my tracks and almost begged me not to go out on the bike she said "I have had this uneasy feeling all night and I saw you hurt please Jeanie don't go on the bike today" but as usual I wouldn't pay any attention to her or the voice in my head.

I just said to her "stop being paranoid I will be ok"! Rolling my eyes and huffing, with that I flounced out of the house and slammed the door!

As I headed out into the city centre enjoying the scenery as I rode along when suddenly I saw in the distance a car driving erratically and very fast somehow I just knew I was going to collide with him even though I slowed down.

I just knew what was going to happen and I couldn't stop it, but somehow things turned into slow motion he hit me and I was flung across the road into a plate glass window, glass shattered everywhere.

I could hear screaming and shouting, everything around me seemed to be going so fast and I seemed to be in slow motion I landed half in half out of the shop window I could see my foot but it was turned at a funny angle and it was near my elbow.

I couldn't feel anything I looked up I saw a sharred piece of glass near my throat people were around me holding me, holding the glass I heard in the distance the sound of bells then blackness came I must have lost consciousness at that point.

I had a very bad accident and had broken many bones in my body especially in my leg and knee I also had internal injuries needless to say it was touch and go but it was while I was been operated on that it happened . . .

The veil started to thin and lift I had this sensation and I saw a wondrous vision,

I was lifted out of my body by the most beautiful white glowing but soft angel she had no wings just a glowing white bright but not glaring light around her I could just make out her face and hair. she was showing me my body lying lifeless on the operating table I didn't hear anything I was a spectator at my own death, I could see the surgeon and the nurses trying to save me putting the paddles on my body seeing the instruments they were using I didn't feel any thingnonly a calm within me then she gently showed me my family who were waiting outside.

I could see my mum holding a plastic white cup and wearing her old red coat and slippers! I saw my brother leaning against the green, blue wall I even saw my mum's husband slumped next to mum with his hands in his pockets

I felt safe and at peace, then she turned me around faced me and spoke to me her voice was like a soft warm breeze on a summers night. but I could hear her clearly she told me that it was not my time and that I had a job to do it was to share my gift and teach about the angels, and not to be afraid of my gift anymore that I would always be protected. She then proceeded to put me back into my lifeless body, all the time I was gazing at her angelic face she then became distant and with a whoosh I was back into my body!

When I came out of intensive care a few weeks later I spoke to my mum and doctor who verified that I had indeed died but the doctor told me my heart was strong and not to worry. I even told my mum about her slippers and red coat and the scene I had seen.

I went on to tell my mum about the angel who came to me also what the angel had said to me but my mum just said "Jeanie anaesthetic plays tricks on you at times you are just lucky and have a strong heart" but my reply to her was "well how did I know what you were wearing on your feet and what I saw?" she took hold of my hand gave it a squeeze and said quietly I don't know.

Needless to say I had a long time thinking about what I had experienced and how I felt and I knew the angel was still around me, protecting me and encouraging me. I could feel their presence it was as if a portal had been opened and they were whispering to me.

As soon as I was well enough I found I had a thirst to learn all about angels and the heavenly realm, my Nanan believed me when I told her she said, "you always had the gift to connect to the angelic realm if they are connecting with you its time you learned" it was then I decided to embrace my gift and learn all I could about the angels.

After this traumatic time my mother seemed to warm to me and accepted me a little more and I started to relax again, even though she was still putting up with the shouting and the darkness that seemed to envelope the house.

I applied to go on an angelology/theology course at the university and started to go to my local spiritual church where I met a wonderful lady who had the gentlest blue eyes and the warmest of smiles calmness seemed to emanate from her and everyone was attracted to her like moths to a flame, she came over to me and hugged me and she said "I know what you have to do" when I looked into her soft eyes I suddenly felt safe, her name was Barbara, she later became my mentor and my dearest friend.

Barbara taught me to be able to channel my visions she told me my angels name There names are Salina also known as "the known one" and Daniel also known as "Danjal" he is also one of the 72 holy angels bearing the name of God, he is also the Archangel of Love. He also works closely with Salina; Daniel is related to the Ascension energies for 3D Earth . . . and is the one "in charge" of the Gates of Ascension.

I had a lot of negative feedback from my mum and some friends when they knew what I was learning I had them scoff at me and they seemed to try their upmost to put me down but it did not deter me from learning. As time went on the friends that I had known started to fall by the way side but were soon replaced with ones that were in infinity with me.

As the years went by I was still learning and absorbing as much as I could, I met my first partner too, and settled into a happy life.

Then came another black time in my life, we had been trying for a family for awhile,

I had miscarriage after miscarriage, I had many tests, examinations at the hospital but I was told by the "experts" I would not be able to carry a child even though Salina and Daniel said I would be blessed with children due to the fact of my injuries from my accident said different.

Daniel also whispered to me that I should name my first born Daniel. Even though at that time I wasn't even pregnant! I started to listen to the whispers that came as I realised they were messages.

This put a real strain on my relationship. My partner started going out a lot and drinking, partying with his friends, I still loved my partner and I just put it down to a blip in our relationship that we would soon overcome, I eventually got pregnant again with the doctors care and family's care I spent weeks and months in the hospital.

My son Daniel was born prematurely and spent some time in hospital as he had jaundice and had to learn to suck, when we brought him home it was the happiest time of my life. Even my partner seemed to settle down and life started to be good again but eighteen months later tragedy struck,

Daniel contracted meningitis by the time I had got to the hospital with him he was so dangerously ill, the doctors tried their best his but death came quickly and he was taken from me, again my faith was tested,

I was alone when Daniel died my partner was out, and couldn't be contacted I found out later he was seeing another woman which turned my world upside down I felt that I had been stabbed twice through the heart! Darkness enveloped me and I couldn't breathe I existed I was on automatic pilot going through the motions of life.

The days were all in darkness to me and I seemed to be consumed in a thickening fog that seemed to trap me I felt that I was a walking dead woman I was alive on the outside but slowly dying on the inside.

He did not even turn up for Daniel's funeral his own son a couple of weeks later, as he had already left me to live with this other woman, I felt so alone and grieving for my son.

After a few months my family encouraged me to start going out again as I was turning into a recluse so with encouragement from friends I eventually started to trust people a few months later I met my husband, little did I know this was the start of another dark time that I would experience.

I soon settled into married life and I was encouraged to have another child from both sides of the family, I became pregnant again with my daughter Kathryn and again my baby was born prematurely (she was due to be born in the middle of January) in November.

She was so tiny and fragile and only weighed 3lb when she was born. I spent every waking time at the hospital praying that she would get stronger and yet again my faith in the angels never wavered. I constantly asked them to protect her and make her strong which they did.

I used to gaze lovingly upon her tiny frame her beautiful black hair, angelic little face with the longest eyelashes that I had ever seen and her tiny hands.

I would put my hand on her back and pray to make her strong.

Even though my marriage was not a happy one my husband liked to drink a lot and I was often left alone and when he eventually came home he was either drunk or smelling of perfume it was like living on a knifes edge, he very rarely worked he was in and out of jobs constantly this put a strain on me not knowing when the next lot of money was going to go in the bank I was working two part-time jobs also studying, both sets of parents were helping looking after Kathryn.

The humiliating thing was that his family and mine helped us frequently and they relished in telling us so, I was so ashamed of him as I tried my up most to improve our lives I was all set to leave him then unbeknown to me I was pregnant a second time, my heart fell but I knew that I could still make a better life with two children I just had to put me leaving on the back burner a little while longer.

My second daughter Claire-Louise was also born prematurely and again I went through the same very testing time indeed. Not only that my dearest Nanan died with a massive heart attack and I never had the chance to say goodbye as I was in hospital so she never really saw Claire-Louise I felt guilty and my heart was broken that I would never see my beloved Nanan again but I know she is with us in spirit and she is by my side to this day she came to me in a dream state and told me that she would be with me and would never leave me.

Unfortunately these times also took a toile on my marriage and it was in ruins I knew I had to get away, get divorced and find a way to make a home for me and my children, somehow I had to get out of the deepest pit my husband had left me with and I had to earn a living, provide for the children and keep a roof over our heads the thought seemed to consume me with fear and in trepidation my confidence level had finally hit rock bottom.

Then one moment of deep despair I had another spiritual experience again I was lifted from my suicidal state and was taken on a journey round the universe, it was Salina who came and said "learn to use your gifts to pass on teach about the angels you have the gift of healing, we will never leave you we are by your side!" I felt the love and the calmness emanate around me.

The next day I woke up refreshed and I decided to follow my spiritual path. The next ten years I had a thirst to learn and find out all I could, I devoted my spare time to learning and connecting to my spirit guides, I wrote down anything and everything that came to me. And whenever I felt down I felt comforted and was urged to carry on by my spirit guides.

I found the inner strength I needed to provide for my children and myself a home. I even managed to take the girls away abroad for the first time in their lives things were starting to settle down and I was finding inner peace at long last.

So my story has started with finding that Spirit guides are evolved beings in the spirit world who usually have had an incarnation in a physical body on planet earth, they volunteer to guide us and help us with our spiritual growth.

This book is how I learned, what I learned, how I evolved into what I am today and my journey to find the inner peace and my lessons that I have learned and trauma I am having to endure to get there And I am still travelling there.

So what's the difference between healing with guides, spiritual healing and angelic healing?

Angels will lift you both to god the healer and the person being healed.

May the Divine Assistance
remain always with you

What are Angels?

People perceive angels in many different ways the most profound encounters are as physical manifestations.

But Angels are genderless beings of a vibration that is pure spirit.

Everyone and everything is made up of vibrations the heavier the vibration, the denser the object

So therefore Angels have a lighter, faster vibration so they are usually invisible to us humans; their male and female qualities are perfect and complete so they are androgynous.

So they are beings beyond the need for sexuality as their masculine and feminine energies is achieved in human beings of either sex, they are beyond sexual desire only the evolved humans reach this level which is why celibacy is very difficult for most humans!

They are high spiritual beings the source (God) appoints angels as guides, protectors and helpers for his creation and uses them as his messengers.

The word 'Angel' means Messenger; Angels are the Messengers of God.

Angels have never existed in human form, nor do humans become angels when they cross over. So the angels' energetic frequencies are calibrated in that humans can sense, feel, hear, see and sometimes even smell them.

Angels bridge our physical reality with their pure spiritual energy that embodies God's perfect love for us. They bridge heaven to earth and create openings—like doorways—to the divine within you.

There are many different kinds of Angels that embody many of aspects of God's love for us. Each Angel serves a different function in your life. Messenger Angels sometimes take on human form for short periods to give you a message or help you with something in your life. A Guardian Angel is a helping, guiding and personal protector Angel that is always looking over you—from before your birth and beyond the time you cross over.

Guardian Angels, or simply angels, are widely believed within Christian theology to be assigned to every person for the duration of their life on earth, providing protection, as well as guidance from the other side. What may shock some is the idea of angels existing around us is not only found within certain religions, but may also find roots within various cultures, too!

Angels also have commonality with spirit guides, benevolent spirits who protect, guide and provide spiritual insight to those on earth. Like angels, they are good spirits believed, to be assigned to a person from birth until death, assisting him or her in their life journey.

Like archangels, they may also appear in a person's life for a short period to bring special guidance and assistance for special concerns. Like when they first appeared to me.

These angels or spirits are believed to be the souls of people who once lived on the earth, but have elevated in consciousness—having evolved unto being enlightened with spiritual wisdom.

Angels are ethereal beings whose primary duties are to assist and to serve God. They act as God's liaison, agent or messenger to life on our planet; in addition to being God's attendants and guardians to humankind. In many ancient scriptures and writings, it is predominantly Angels that carry out the will of God.

What's particularly interesting when I was studying the Angels, there are certain similarities to other beings, Not-Of-This-Earth, as found in the myths and legends of other cultures. Were their gods and goddesses really what we have come to know and call Angels? Could it be that our ancient predecessors were more sensitive to the supernatural than we are?

If Angels are close to humanity, do we come in touch with them on a regular basis, only not to see them? Certainly the billions of people who adhere to a devout belief in today's structured religions, combined with the billions of previous inhabitants of our planet, cannot be wrong. ANGELS REALLY DO EXIST!

Many ask, "How can I recognize an Angel?" The most important first step to "tuning in" to an Angelic presence is as simple as it may be difficult. YOU MUST BELIEVE THAT ANGELS EXIST!

If you cannot bring yourself to acknowledge their existence and reality, one can only hope they feel that your life-purpose is important enough for them to reveal themselves to you. In fact, when reviewing the many recounts of Angelic appearances, it seems that Angels materialize most frequently when and where they are needed. Then, they mysteriously disappear or become invisible.

It's particularly interesting that the form most people associate Angels with is the traditional Angel with wings and a Halo. Some say the wings are to identify them as a Spirit and to emphasize their role as a messenger.

To the best of our knowledge, Angels reported in the Bible never appeared this way. Nor did they ever appear as plump bare little children with mini-wings. They always appear as full-grown adults. Keep in mind however, that when they do appear, their purpose is to help us and guide us. Not to shock us into having a major heart attack!

Angels will appear as humans who are so beautiful or handsome that our thoughts prevent us from recognizing them as an Angel, We are mesmerized!

In essence, they can appear in virtually any form they choose whether it be human or animal. Angels are essentially "Spirits" and are not dependant on a physical body as we humans are. They can be visible or invisible, auditory only, unseen and unheard but "felt."

They have the freedom to assume any form necessary in order to accomplish their mission. When they are not in the physical form, there are different ways to tell if you are in the presence of an Angel. Often the smell of flowers or another pleasing natural scent will accompany their presence usually vanilla or jasmine.

Sometimes an Angel will announce its presence with a slight breeze even if all the windows are all closed! The breeze is believed to be the "flutter" of their wings.

Sometimes you may hear a faint or distant sound of Bells, chimes, or trumpets. Even in your dreams you may sense they are around you and you may actually see them in your "dream state"

We have continued to be impressed by the remarkable adaptability of the guardian angels. In one instance, an angel could be the fireman who carried smoke inhalation victims to safety and who later cannot be found by grateful survivors. Or it could be the woman who has helped someone to believe in life again by just giving a kind word, Then never to be seen again.

Of one thing we are certain: If an angel should appear to you, you will perceive the heavenly messenger in a way most acceptable and understandable to you.

In the angelic realm the heavenly hosts are arranged into groups according to their abilities, duties, and responsibilities. I will try my best to explain how they are arranged.

These groups are on different levels or tiers within the celestial realm.

The highest tier at the top are the angelic beings called SERAPHIM these beings are composed of pure white light. Below the seraphim are the CHERUBIM; There duty is to care for the stars and heavenly lights this second order of angels also serve as keepers of the AKASHIC RECORDS.

The Akashic records are like a library where all knowledge of human experience and the history of the cosmos are kept each soul has its own Akashic record its own library of life.

Below the cherubim are a group of angels known as OPHANIM or THRONES and these angels act as cosmic judges.

Reigning over the next tier are the celestial "managers" who keep the universe running smoothly, these angels are called the DOMINIONS.

Then we come to the VIRTUES these are the ones that can work miracles here on earth and they also have the power to bestow the most important "virtues" on man kind such as courage, wisdom, compassion, etc.

Underneath the virtues is a group of angels named the POWERS these angels protect the universe.

The third tier is the one that is closest to us this is why the angels on this level are so concerned with what happens to the earth and us. These angels also interact with humans.

This tier are called the PRINCIPILITIES (or princes)

Next come the ARCHANGELS their duties include guarding all nature as well as humanity these angels are considered the most important of the heavenly messengers the ones that is so well known is ARCHANGEL MICHAEL, RAPHAEL, GABRIEL, and URIEL.

And below them are the GUARDIAN angels that watch over each and every one of us.

The Seven Heavens

Although angels exist in every dimension they are traditionally thought to inhibit seven heavens this is a belief also to the monotheistic religious traditions such as Islam, Christianity and Judaism the seventh heaven is where God dwells.

The seven heavens are spiritual realms and many of the names can be found in the Old Testament.

The FIRST heaven is called VILLON but it also known as SHAMAYMIM this is the lowest heaven and is associated with the planetary angels and angels that rule the stars and the atmosphere, wind and water.

Archangel Gabriel rules the first heaven and it is said to be the paradise where Adam and Eve first dwelt and where the tree of life and knowledge grow.

The SECOND heaven is known some times as a holding place for sinners awaiting the day of judgement this heaven is called RAQIA the zodiac angels rule over this sphere raqia is also the dwelling place for John the Baptist in Islamic tradition and this heaven is ruled over by Archangel Raphael and Zachariel.

The THIRD heaven is called SHECHAKIM this is a strange heaven as hell is found in its northern region and a river of flame flows through it and it is here that the wicked is punished the angel who rules over this domain is called Anahel with the help of Jagniel, Rabacyle and Dalquiel (the three princes) in the southern half lies a paradise a garden that has a gate of gold (the famous pearly gates) through which all perfected souls pass two rivers flow through it one of milk and honey and the other of oil and wine.

The FOURTH heaven is called ZEBHUL and this is ruled over by Archangel Michael this is where the Alter and the Temple of God lies, it is the city of Christ this city is made of gold and has twelve walls encircling it and twelve walls within these walls also have twelve gates that are rich in beauty.

The FIFTH heaven is called MACHON and Archangel Sandolphon rules this heaven, this is where vast choirs sing gods praises day and night also some of the fallen angels are also held there.

The SIXTH heaven is called MAKON and The Angel Zachiel rules this heaven, this is also where the Akashic records are kept and stored these record all happenings on earth including the deeds of every individual who has ever lived on earth as well as their punishment or reward.

The SEVENTH heaven is called ARABOTH and it is ruled by Cassiel the angel of solitude and tears, This angel is one of the angels that also rules over Saturn It is the abode of the holiest and the highest order of angels, Seraphim, cherubim, and thrones dwell there it is also the home of the blessed spirits and the unborn souls.

Connecting with the Angels

We are too distracted by our physicality and the world around us to connect with the higher dimensions in which angels reside. Suffice it to say that because of our physicality, we are cut off from connecting with these higher beings. That does not mean that such connections cannot be made.

It simply means that we need to move beyond our physical limitations in order to find those connections. Angels and guides are 'out there,' so Suffice it to say that because of our physicality, we are cut off from connecting with these higher beings. That does not mean that such connections cannot be made.

It simply means that we need to move beyond our physical limitations in order to find those connections. Angels and guides are 'out there,' so to speak, and are always trying to communicate with us.

Here is a tip on how you may be able to connect to your angel guide.

Once comfortably seated, close your eyes and take some deep breaths to get relaxed. Focus on your breath. When thoughts come streaming into consciousness, bring your focus back to breathing in and breathing out.

No need to strain the breath. Just breathe. As you become more relaxed, your thoughts will become weaker. In any event, don't worry too much about them. Thinking is what the mind does all day and night, too.

We cannot stop thinking on the conscious level, but as we allow ourselves to get more relaxed and access the more subtle parts of the mind, thought thins out, so to speak, and eventually disappears, leaving us with pure consciousness.

A helpful technique is to simply ask your mind not to bother you; to just remain quiet and observe what you are doing during this session.

Picture putting your mind off to one side, for instance say on a pillow or a cushion. Thank your mind for cooperating in this fashion. Should any thoughts disrupt your meditation at any time, remind the mind that it is only suppose to observe and not interfere, and put it back on the pillow or cushion. Thank it again for being cooperative. When you feel yourself completely relaxed, try to picture a white or yellow light coming from your solar plexus.

The solar plexus is that place just below the breast, at the upper section of the abdomen. It represents your intuitive powers Picture the light moving upward and outward from this area. It should move out and swirl around you, engulfing you. This may take more than one meditative session to learn to do, but continue working on it.

After two, three or perhaps more days, you hopefully will have a handle on it. When you are able to see the light moving upward and swirling around you, without strain, then you are ready for the next step.

One note of caution here: sometimes the light may be bright and sometimes not. Some days you may even have a difficult time seeing the light at all. But as long as it is in your awareness, that is enough. Do not try to strain or force anything.

The next step is to imagine a triangle that looks like a diamond sitting in the centre of your solar plexus, inside the light. The tip of the diamond rises to your upper chest, just below your throat. See if you can visualize how bright it is and how it gleams, the way diamonds do.

In time, the diamond may grow larger inside of you. Also, in time, you may see the bright shine of the diamond radiating out from you and engulfing you, too. You may possibly see someone inside the diamond, or it may be you inside the diamond.

Keep this meditative technique up. Do it two or three times a day. Generally, each session takes about ten to fifteen minutes. Different experiences will grow out of this over time, and one day you may find yourself making contact with a higher being.

Many people say they can't *meditate,* because they can't still their minds. When they sit down to meditate, their minds just race on . . . .

and on . . . . and on . . . . Well, you are not alone!

There are many different forms of meditation, such as **yantra, mantra and chakra,** they all use concentration techniques to help us stop thinking and relax our brains. Meditation, Relaxation and visualization are our starting points.

We always work within a spiritual context, using meditation to build a bridge to the invisible worlds. With all the physical and loud noises and distractions in the world, it is hard to focus inside us and truly feel peace and quiet.

Only through this sort of focus can we truly concentrate on our spiritual communications with guides and our inner intuition.

For example, how many times have you shut your eyes to go to sleep and suddenly fallen into a complete state on relaxation without thinking: "what's for dinner tomorrow or shall I do the ironing or something similar" There are a number of ways to do this and as time goes by, you will probably be able to create your own.

Empty your mind (this will be very hard at first, but with some practice you should achieve it.) You Can Imagine a ball on pure white energy in the centre of your body, it slowly grows and grows until it has encompassed the whole of you full and at peace and relaxed.

Or visualise a beautiful door visualise yourself standing in front of a door—any kind of door is OK, as long as you like it—it could be a big old castle-door, a beautiful oak-carved door, an ultra-modern looking door—or any other kind of door you can think of.

Now Ask the question, Then Imagine that behind this door is the answer to a question you want to know the answer to—the question doesn't have to be a problem in the negative sense of the word, it could be a question about something good. Now, mentally, ask your question.

Visualise the door opening, as you visualise the door slowly opening, imagine a white light beaming through it. As it opens wider and wider visualise more and more brilliant white light pouring out of it,

Centre yourself; then allow the answer to come to you. As you stand there, bathed in the white light streaming through the door, allow thoughts to come to you. It doesn't matter how absurd these thoughts may appear to be, just let them come to you.

Protection from Negative Energy

People in our lives connect to us with psychic energetic cords. These are usually people that we have had intimate moments and/or contact with (good friends, family or lovers), which allows them to stay in your energy field.

It is important to remove the cords of the people we no longer want to have attached to us anymore, so that their energy will not stay entangled in our own.

Anyone can attach to anyone at any given moment, even the person that drives by you and yells at you in traffic can connect to you with a black chord, and they too need to be released daily to prevent future health problems

Psychic Protection

These notes are only guidelines to aid you on your own Spiritual path and as with all spiritual work it is often about finding your own Truth. If you disagree or feel uncomfortable with anything that is suggested here by all means find an alternative Truth that is acceptable to you.

Psychic protection is one of the most important parts of psychic work. Embarking on a psychic journey can make you more sensitive to other people's Negativity, and anything else that feel like draining your energy

SAY A LITTLE PRAYER: Now you do not have to be religious for this to apply. However, you want to invoke protection no matter whatever your faith is. I am not a particularly religious person myself; however, this is the prayer I use:

> I humbly ask for protection To protect me
> Also everyone around me on all levels.
> I ask for the heavenly rays to be poured upon me in
> abundance.
> I ask for the Highest and Brightest,
> My Spiritual loved ones, friends, and guides to come
> forward To Educate, Guide and protect me on all levels,
> I ask this in your name.

Anyone can attach to anyone at any given moment, even the person that drives by you and yells at you in traffic can connect to you with a black chord, and they need to be released daily to prevent future health problems.

You can do the following:

Meditate and call in your spirit guides or angels and visualize all the black cords or whatever you feel is connecting you. Ask your spirit guides or angels to help you disconnect to anyone who has sent you negative energy in any shape or form.

Ask that all negative connections be broken. Picture all the cords or webs attached into your body. Imagine a giant pair of scissors and cut all the black cords. Or better yet, picture yourself pulling those cords out by their very roots. Some roots go deep. Pull hard and do it with intention.

It is also important to close down properly too when you have meditated or had contact with your angels to stop any negativity chords, entities damaging your chakras, your psychic field

This is the prayer I use to close down to protect myself . . .

CLOSING DOWN

Heavenly Father, Divine Mother
Thank You for Bringing My Guides and Helpers Forward
To Help Me Along With My Spiritual Path
Once Again I Ask for Your Protective Cloak, Surrounded
in Bright White Light Only
from the highest level In Your Name

Which is Love

Asking an Angel for help is one of our most powerful spiritual practices. We can ask the Angels for immediate help at any time and in any place.

Angels work with everyone regardless of personal histories and beliefs.

When you want or need help from your angels, all you have to do is simply ask. Nothing you do, say, think or feel can ever make your angels leave your side.

Take notice of any feelings or sensations you get, as well as any images, sounds, or thoughts that come to you. These could be your angels trying to reach you Meditate. Many people think that meditation is a skill that they can obtain only by taking expensive courses or spending years with a guru.

Actually, meditation is as simple as closing your eyes and listening. Don't worry about what posture you are in or if New Age music is playing in the background.

Simply get into a comfortable position, close your eyes and try to free your mind. When a thought bubbles up, just push it away.

Don't get uptight about the fact that thoughts will occur; your brain was made to think and it's going to provide thoughts whether you like it or not. Just keep brushing away the extraneous thoughts until you feel tranquil. This may only last fifteen minutes. Keep working at it until you can sustain long periods of peacefulness.

Listen. You will hear your own mind chattering away, but you might also hear something else—a voice that's not your own. Instead of immediately assuming, it's your imagination, cherish the voice. Let it through. Soon you'll be hearing more!

To be able to connect we need to raise (and keep rising) our own vibration to sense the angels around us easily we do this by self healing and meditation also clearing away blockages. Let the angels become your friend try to work with them everyday and you will find yourself moving further towards love and light, believe me the journey is an angelic one indeed.

As I said before that angels have a higher vibration than us earthly beings but as you deepen your angelic connection you will gradually sense their energy in your heart, hands and atmosphere around you.

All angels have a specific role to play basically they have a job to do there is angels who care for the Seasons, days of the week, Planets, Zodiac even your Chakras. As you get to know the wisdom of the angels your life will begin a transformation a sort of healing and you will start to look at things in a different light with new fresh eyes!

The First Huge Hurdle

A s I was learning all about the Angels and the roles they did and what they could do for us my life was beginning to pan out and everything seemed to be fitting into place my daughters were growing into beautiful teenagers and I was starting to feel contented.

Then one day it abruptly came to a standstill with a check-up some time before at the hospital, I received the letter from the hospital asking me to go back to see the consultant, I decided not to tell the girls as it could be nothing and I didn't want to worry them unduly.

I felt uneasiness as I entered the hospital I immediately smelt the clinical atmosphere and just put my uneasiness down to nerves.

I went to the reception, gave my details and then sat down to wait for my name to be called I glanced at the table of magazines and picked one up without really looking at what it was as my mind was in a whirl, when I did look at the magazine it was an old fate and destiny magazine and I opened straight away onto a page talking about angels.

I started to read not really taking in the words and then a familiar voice in my ear said "be strong you will be ok", suddenly I was called in to see the consultant I listened to what he had to say to me as I sat in front of him determined to be professional and ask all the questions that had been going round my head but when I tried nothing came out of my mouth and yet in my head was screaming "NO not me you have got it wrong"!.

When I came out of the consultants room I was in

a daze the nurse asked me if I wanted a cup of tea and had I brought someone with me, I just shook my head and sat down dumbstruck, my body felt numb but in my head questions and answers were whirling round like a washing machine on fast spin.

I sat that felt like hours I finished my cup of tea and calmly got up and decided that I would tell my daughters and just have faith in my angel, when I arrived home I calmly set about making the tea listening to the sounds of the girls music and them chatting and the blaring of the TV of the local news. All the time in my head I was rehearsing what I was going to say to them, how was I going to tell them without scaring them to bits!

After tea I asked Katie and Claire to stay a little while before they ran off to carry on what they were doing before. I asked for a little of their time I picked up my cup of tea and sat down in the lounge, they followed me asking "what's wrong mum".

I told them that I had been to the hospital that morning and that I had received some results that had not been very good I was greeted with "why mum why didn't you tell us that you had gone we would have come with you"!

It was this remark that made me cry and through my tears and my body was shaking from head to toe I finally plucked up the courage to say the word Cancer, Claire burst into tears and then Katie they both rushed into my arms and then we just clung together in a huddle as if we were never ever going to see each other again!

When we all finally calmed down I told them what the consultant had told me that I had to have a hysterectomy and intensive chemotherapy it was then I felt my angel's envelope us all in their arms.

I said to the girls have hope and faith I shall fight and I was not ready to die yet then I got a barrage of questions such as "we will help you mum"! "You have got to rest", and "who will look after us while you are in hospital"? "We have to tell the family"! With each question that came out I gave them the answer that they wanted and needed to hear.

The next morning I woke up and I still felt numb from yesterday's events as I looked up at the ceiling in my bedroom looking at how the reflection of the sun danced on my light shade making little rainbow colours.

As I laid in bed I decided that how I was going to tackle this problem was to meet it head on and to organise things and prepare everyone and myself included for the forthcoming operation and treatments it was this point that I asked Daniel and Salina to help shore up my strength and courage also to protect my children too.

The girls did not want to go to school and leave me but I insisted that they went and said "we are just going to carry on as normal for now" so with glum faces I drove them to school and promised them that I would pick them up after school then we would have a treat and go out for tea.

When I arrived home I just stood and looked around me drinking in the scene of scattered clothes, slippers just tossed into the box that was on the floor the morning dishes that were just put on the side ready for washing I glanced at myself in the mirror my face was etched with worry and I looked pale it was as if I was looking at this stranger yet I knew her very well,

My dog Penny was wagging her tail and she licked my hand as if to say "hey I am here"! Which then brought me back to the now so I sat down on the settee and let the tears flow, all the time penny sat looking at me with her big brown eyes with concern in them pawing me. After I had cried all the tears that I could i felt my angel again and she said in my ear "this is another test you can be strong we will help you, you still have work to do"

I replied "yes I know please just tell me what to do", I dried my eyes washed my face tackled the house chores as if it was just another ordinary day, luckily it was my day off from work which was a saving grace as I knew I couldn't have been able to face the staff or the children I had a job teaching in a special needs school, and the children would have picked up on that I was not well, and would have asked questions.

I made myself a cup of tea and with a pad and pencil I decided to make a list with penny curled up by my side she seemed to sense that I needed her with me. First I would have to tell all the family including my ex-husband as he needed to know for the sake of the girls.

What better time to do it was there and then. So I picked up the phone and rang all the necessary people of course I was greeted with are you sure? When? Where? And how, and I am coming over right now!

So with gentle reassuring I told them I was ok and I would see them at the weekend with the girls. I felt totally wrecked and tired out but the strength was coming from somewhere for me to get things done and organised.

I closed my eyes and drifted off to sleep and while I slept my angels came to me they took my hands and held them I felt all the love and energy flow from them into me I was bathed in a pure white light.

I was then guided into a temple it was very beautiful glittering gold and luminous with all the colours of the rainbow emanating from inside as we entered I was greeted by the other spirits,

My dad, my nana and they all wrapped their arms around me it felt very comforting almost like a soft warm blanket and I felt very safe and loved I didn't want to leave.

Then I was taken back to my body as I woke up from my slumber I knew I had been to the temple on the fourth heaven, they had taken me to show me that I was being cared for and being looked after and I would have the strength from all the angels to help fight this cancer.

I prayed and thanked all the angels around me for showing me, helping me to get through this ordeal.

Later that day I picked the girls up from school and we decided to go to the All American diner for tea as we sat waiting to be served with our meal the girls asked me how I felt and what I was going to do obviously it had been playing on their minds too.

So I told them what I had done and who I had chatted to we chatted about school, boys, fashion, what lessons they had that day. We kept the conversation light and easy while we ate our huge burgers and fries and listened to Elvis playing in the background.

With it being a Friday the girls would normally go out with their friends but the girls decided they wanted to stay with me which I was glad of as having them with me felt very precious. When we arrived home I was ordered to sit down and they made me a cup of tea they tidied their rooms and busied themselves in the kitchen. later that evening they came in with a tray of sweets, biscuits, crisps, nibbles and we all snuggled up on the sofa, dog included to watch the TV.

As I looked at both my girls on either side of me I knew I was never going to let a little thing like Cancer beat me and take me away from my precious little family.

My eyes started to well up again so with a deep breathe I swallowed the feeling and held on to both my daughters until it passed, later that night when I was in bed I thanked the angels and asked God to look after my girls while I was busy fighting my battle and to give them the strength to cope with my illness as I was drowning into a deep sleep.

I felt a hand stroke my head and I heard my father's voice in my ear "I will never leave you Jeanie" it felt comforting and I felt a calm within me,

I woke up the next day with both the girls beside me, they must have crept into my bed during the night . . . it was very comforting to see them curled up asleep beside me their long blonde hair tumbled about on the pillow and listening to their soft breathing in and out I just lay there and silently said "thank you God for giving me two beautiful daughters that I love dearly".

As the day of the operation approached I felt very calm and knew that I had everything in place for the girls and that they understood what was happening and what they had to do.

Everyone rallied round and I just kept myself busy until the actual day dawned. That morning I woke up and being surprisingly calm I jumped into the shower checked through that I had everything for the hospital my friend called to take me to the hospital the girls insisted that they came too which I didn't mind I just needed them around me at that time.

We arrived on the ward and I was met by a nice warm hearted nurse who ushered me to my bed and explained to me what I had to do, after I said my good byes to the girls and my friend and reassured them that I was ok so with lots of hugging and crying and wiping of tears they left me, the nurse came back and with a smile.

She started to asked me the obligatory questions which I answered I felt I was on automatic pilot and I was living a nightmare and that I was going to wake up and realise that it was a dream. But I knew I was not I was shaking inside and felt numb from head to toe but I had to be strong and silently I prayed and asked for that strength,

A few hours later I woke up and the operation had been done I felt so ill and felt as if I was in a deep pit and couldn't get out I was shouting and no one was hearing me and it was in this deepest despair that my angel came to me again I felt a warmth flow through me and felt my father stroking my head even my nan came through it's as if they knew I needed them all there to help me get through the nightmare the pain in my body subsided and I fell back into a dreamless sleep.

As the days went by my mind and body started to get a little stronger the doctors said that I was making good recovery and that I would start the chemotherapy straight away and that I would have it intravenously.

So I was hooked up to wires and tubes it was also explained to me that I would feel sick and very tired my moods would change I asked all the questions including the one "would I lose my hair"? The response from the doctors was "you may lose your hair but it depends on how your body reacts to the chemicals"

The thought of having chemicals put into my body filled me with dread so when my friends came to see me I asked them to find natural alternative ways that could help defeat the cancer the doctor also reassured me that the operation had been successful and that chemotherapy was a necessary precaution as there could be some cancerous cells still there.

So with trepidation I began the gruelling chemotherapy and true to form the sickness came also the moods but also came the nightmares my body clock was all over the place and my hair started to fall out in clumps my skin felt dry, itchy and yet I looked grey with dark shadows under my eyes the family were constantly by my side and when the pain became really bad which was mostly during the night.

I prayed and prayed that my angels helped me and they did I felt the calm and the strength seeping through me like a warm blanket being wrapped around me and it was only then that I felt the blessed sleep come to me.

As the days went on I was eventually discharged from hospital and was allowed to go home I was then put into the care of the MacMillan nurses they came to see me every day and checked that I was being good!

I got to know the nurses who became very good friends Margaret and Susan they said they used to leave me till last as they used to love coming for a cup of tea and a chat! As the days turned into months I eventually recovered, my hair started to grow back and I started to see the light once more, again I had recovered from the deepest pit of despair and again my faith in my angels never wavered I had past yet another test of life crossed the road onto another new road what would this road lead to?

I had faith in my angels because they said I would recover and I did Salina and Daniel said I still had work to do so with new energy and thirst I began to study once more.

The Archangels

There are seven angels who stand before the Divine source in the book of Revelations and these angels are considered to be the greatest archangels their names are Michael, Gabriel, Raphael, Auriel, Raguel, Sariel, and Remiel as you will note all the angels name end with el this is significant as it means the shining being the first four that were mentioned above are also known as the four great angels of presence, however there are lots of archangels too many to mention so I will only mention the main ones

Michael traditionally pronounced MEE-Kay-ehl. Michael is the best known archangel he is the protector of the churches his name means "who is like the divine source" and Michael is believed to be the closest to the divine source

Michael is also known as the divine protector of the world and it is said that he will show himself if the world is in danger he is also the archangel of protection and balance and works to bring patience and protection against any psychic imbalances or danger,

Michael also represents LOVE and his element is FIRE his direction is SOUTH and the season that he protects is

AUTUMN, his colour is RED and the zodiac signs are ARIES, LEO, and SAGITTARIUS.

The crystal most often associated with Michael is SUGALITE it is said by wearing this crystal you can become more open to receiving messages and protection from him. Michael's aura is royal blue mixed with tinges of purple and silver when he is near you, you may experience flashes of cobalt blue sparkles of light.

Michael will help you release fear so if you become worried or fearful, depressed all you have to do is ask Michael to release these things to him, and he will assist you to bring peace and tranquillity back to your life.

Gabriel traditionally known as GAH-bree-ehl, Gabriel sits on the left hand side of the divine source and is considered to be the second most important archangel. Gabriel is usually pictured as female and the name Gabriel also means "the divine source is my strength"

Gabriel has a strong connection to pregnancy and birth and is considered to be the divine source's envoy to humankind she is also the archangel of hope, love and illumination and guards the sacred places of the world and the sacred waters of life she is also the messenger angel.

Gabriel helps with teaching of spiritual duties including within us a better understanding of our dreams Gabriel represents OVERCOMING DOUBT her element is WATER her direction is WEST and her season is WINTER her zodiac signs that she represents are CANCER, SCORPIO, and PISCES her crystal gem is EMERALD

She will also help you with any writing or correspondences helping you deliver healing messages Gabriel's aura is copper and Citrine wearing either of these will help you to connect with Gabriel.

Raphael traditionally known as RAH-phay-ehl is the third most important archangel he is the keeper of the Holy Grail his name means "shining one who heals" Raphael is known to help heal the wounds of martyrs and he is the protector of travellers he is the archangel of healing and by working with him he helps to stimulate the energy of healing within us

Raphael represents HEALING his element is AIR his direction is EAST the season that he looks after is SPRING his colour is GREEN and the zodiac signs he represents are GEMINI, AQUARIUS, LIBRA

When asking for help with he will often answer you in intuitive thoughts, dreams, ideas so be aware of the subtle information that comes through to you when he offers his healing light and love to any situation you will often feel or see the emerald green energy around that situation.

Auriel also known as Uriel traditionally known as HOUR-eee-ehl/YOUR-eee-ehl this angel is the fourth and final archangel of the four angels of the presence, her name means "fire or light of the divine source"

Auriel is known as the angel of repentance and it is this angel who meets the souls of sinners, as they arrive in heaven Auriel is also the angel of music and is the angel of alchemy and vision. She is also the tallest of the angels that has eyes that can see all over eternity

She also works with the nature spirits and works to assist humanity by awakening humanity to the nature spirits working with her will open you to the fairy and other nature kingdoms.

Auriel represents CLEAR THINKING her element is EARTH and her direction is NORTH her season is SUMMER and her colour is WHITE OR PALE YELLOW the zodiac signs she looks after are TAURUS, VIRGO and CAPRICORN her energy is strongly aligned with AMBER and by wearing amber it will assist you to connect with her energy.

Raguel traditionally known as RAH-guh-ehl, the name Raguel means "friend of the divine source" Raguel's "job" is to oversee that the other angels maintain high standards of behaviour he is also known as the angel of ice and snow when your faith wavers or your spirits are low call upon Raguel to help you because just as Raguel oversees the angels and archangels to assure harmony, order and cooperation he also assists humans to sort out our feelings which then enables us to understand and follow our feelings.

Raguel's colour is a beautiful PALE BLUE like the colour of the sky in a summer morning his gemstone is AQUAMARINE by wearing this you will be able to align yourself with his wisdom and kindness.

Sariel also known as Haniel traditionally known as SAHR-eee-ehl and HAHN-eee-ehl Sariel means the way of the divine source and Haniel's name means glory of the divine Sariel is a healer very much like Raphael but with the added distinction of being the angel who is most able to heal and work with those who have moved away from the path of light and the divine Sariel/

Haniel will assist you further to realize your higher potential by assisting you to work with your hidden talents and to polish your skills.

He will also assist you to honour your natural cycles, moods, rhythm's and to embrace every part of ourselves whether this be strengths or shadows.

Sariel/Haniel's aura is BLUE-WHITE like the moons full glow his gemstone that is associated to him is the MOONSTONE which has magical nurturing energy, wear or hold the moonstone when you wish to connect with Sariel/Haniel this caring and nurturing can affect miracles within and for you.

Remiel/Jeremiel traditionally known as REH-mee-ehl or JUH-reh- mee-ehl this angel is known as the angel of hope and his task is leading the souls to heaven and he also leads us back to realization of our spiritual self. The name means the divine source rises up or mercy of the divine.

Remiel/Jeremiel will also assist you to have a more merciful outlook and this will enable you to consistently treat yourself with respect and tender loving care, he can also help you to review where you have been, what you have learned or what was available to be learned, what recurring patterns you are ready to release and what there is to be grateful for in your life.

His aura is a very DEEP PURPLE and when he is around you may experience sparkles of bright purple the crystal/gemstone associated with Remiel is AMYTHEST By wearing amethyst it will bring you closer to his energy.

Chamuel traditionally known as CHAM-you—ehl his name means "he who sees the divine source" Chamuel has the ability to help assist you to find things, situations and people who are integral to our soul's mission he also assists us to drop judgmental attitudes towards others and to develop a more tolerant view of our own shortcomings,

When you work with Chamuel you will experience a pleasant loving excitement because he sees your true qualities and loves you unconditionally, Chamuel's aura is a PALE GREEN like a new born leaf in spring his crystal/gemstone is GREEN FLUORITE by wearing this gemstone you will feel his loving energy around you.

Zadkiel traditionally known as ZHAD-kee-ehl his name means the righteousness of the divine source he is also known as the angel of mercy. Zadkiel is a spiritual professor he is patient and kind and has access to ALL knowledge.

Anything that you wish to know Zadkiel can bring you he is also known for his ability to assist humans with memory, if you have the need to remember or trying to memorize ask Zadkiel to assist you.

Zadkiel will also work with you to clear away any emotional toxins from your heart to effect emotional healings which may occur in miraculous ways he will also remind us to open our hearts and minds in gratitude for all that we have at present because only when we are grateful for what we have and where we are will the divine source bring even more to us.

Zadkiel's aura is a DEEP INDIGO BLUE and the gemstone/crystal that is associated to him is LAPIS LAZULI by holding this stone above your third eye while calling on his assistance you open yourself more fully to the divine source.

Raziel traditionally known as RAW-zee-ehl his name means the secrets of the divine source. Raziel is the angel that assists us to understand esoteric spiritual ideas and then further incorporate them into our everyday physical life in practical ways he is also known as the alchemist of the angelic realm as he helps us to understand ideas which defy logical thinking, He can also assist you to turn your ideas and intuitions into reality.

If you are longing, hungering for spiritual help and understanding ask Raziel to enter your dreams he will then take you on a journey to places of learning where he will work with you to enable to discover truths and secrets don't worry that you may not remember all when you have woken it will still be imbedded in your subconscious where it will guide you through out your daily life.

Raziel's aura holds all the colours of the RAINBOW and his gemstone /crystal is CLEAR QUARTZ as you look through the crystal you may see reflections of all the colours this helps magnify your own natural clairvoyance and will assist you in feeling closer to Raziel and in understanding the secrets he will bring to you if you but ask.

Jophiel traditionally known as JAW-phee-ehl she is also known as Iophiel and Zophiel her name means beauty of the divine source.

She is also the angel of paradise and is the patron angel of artists as well as being the angel of illumination. Jophiel will assist us in keeping our space clear whether it is within or without, if you feel cluttered within or confused call upon her to spring clean and bring peace.

Jophiel also sees the beauty in everything and everyone and she will help you see the beauty in all things around you. She will assist you with finding more grace and peace in our lives by slowing down and noticing the beauty around us, she loves the outdoors and nature.

Jophiel wants us to savour each and every moment in our lives rather than looking outward or to something in the future to bring us happiness by calling on Jophiel she will assist you to increase your awareness and appreciation of the everyday miracles of life.

Jophiel's aura is a DEEP ROSE PINK which signifies her compassionate and caring nature her gemstone/ crystal is PINK RUBILITE by wearing this it brings forth her energy to you.

Azrael traditionally known as AS-rah-ehl this angels name means whom the divine source assists. Azrael is concerned with assisting those who are themselves "helpers "as well as assisting humans to transition from the earthly plane. He helps humans who are at a loss, despair and those who feel that they have nothing to live for,

Azrael works very closely with those who have transitioned from the earthly plane so calling on this angel he may bring a message or a dream visitation from your loved ones who have passed over. If you call upon Azrael to help guide your words and actions during sessions and counselling others he will assist you in bringing more patience and compassion.

Azrael's aura is a beautiful shade of CREAM-VANILLA CREAM with YELLOW UNDERTONES he will envelope those in transition with this loving cream light to bring them comfort and peace.

When Azrael is around you may see EGG SHELL-COLOURED twinkling lights in the room. His gemstone/crystal is the CREAMY YELLOW CALCITE this stone is most calibrated to Azrael's energy and holding this stone or having it in the area will assist in bringing extra comfort.

Ariel traditionally known as AHR-eee-ehl her name means lioness of the divine source she is a reflection of bravery, courage focus and elegant movement if you see images or feel lions or lionesses near you this is a sign she is with you if you need courage or confidence with any situation or assistance with standing up for your beliefs call upon Ariel who will then gently but firmly guide you to be courageous and stand up for your convictions.

Ariel is especially supportive of those who are healers, teachers and service workers she is also known as the Angel of the Earth and is patron of all the wild animals and is this guise supervises the realm of the nature spirits such as Fairies Elves, Leprechauns, which are also known as nature angels.

Ariel and her earth angels can help us understand the natural rhythms of the earth and to experience the magical healing properties of rocks trees and plants she also works to help heal and look after all animals especially those who live in water.

Ariel's aura is a pale shade of PINK and her gemstone/crystal is PINK QUARTZ ask her for what you need and she will guide you however remember to put aside your earthly expectations as they only serve you only to limit what Ariel is able can bring into your life.

Sandolphon traditionally known as SAN-dahl-fon his name means brother he is also the angel of prayer and Master of the angelic song. He is also the patron angel of music, Sandolphon is one of the two Archangels who were mortal men and who lived such remarkable spiritual lives that they ascended to the Archangelic Kingdom. Sandolphon can assist you to live and build your life to be a masterpiece, ask him to assist you to live in integrity with all your spiritual gifts of healing, prophecy and manifestation.

He will also help you to only speak the truth that will benefit all. One of the roles that Sandolphon does is that he will deliver any prayers and affirmations he will also work with us when we need to receive more. Sandolphon will also assist you to find a calm centre from which your words and actions will be kind and gentle yet extremely powerful.

He will also act as a guide when you need advice in communication and he will always guide you and assist you to find the right path for your highest good. Sandolphon's aura is a calming shade of TURQUOISE just like the colour of the ocean; his gemstone/crystal is the TURQUOISE and by meditating on this stone you may feel a deep sense of calm and your breathing will become slow and your heart rate will drop to an extremely calm state of wellbeing.

You may sense that Sandolphon is around you by the sense of calmness also you may hear music or singing.

Metatron traditionally known as MATE-ah-tron his name means the one who occupies the throne next to the divine source. Metatron is also the angel of the covenant as well as the patron angel of small children he is said to be the king of the angels and he is the twin brother of Sandolphon.

He was also the angel that was mortal and was said to be called Enoch in his earthly incarnation. Metatron also works closely with psychic and sensitive children and his beloved children who have agreed to come to Earth now called the Indigo or Crystal children.

Metatron will assist humans to develop organizational and record keeping skills if you call upon him he will help you to organise your priorities. On a day to day basis Metatron is extremely adept at assisting us to cleanse and balance our chakras and our aura so call upon him when you feel the need to be cleansed.

Metatron's aura is a DEEP BEAUTIFUL VIOLET with SUBTLE SEA GREEN STRIPES his gemstone/crystal is WATERMELON TOURMALINE. If you feel the need to connect with Metatron meditate with this stone to connect to his energy.

Another Hurdle

As I was studying hard and trying to work to keep a roof over mine and the children's head things started to fall into a routine, the girls used to see their father on a regular basis, the trouble was every time they went to see him they would come back looking glum and sometimes upset or angry and I would be on tender hooks wondering what he would be telling them next.

I often used to ask the angels to protect the girls when they visited him but as time went on Katie started to believe him and I was always the butt of her anger her respect for me at the time was starting to wane and I found it increasingly difficult to connect with her wave length.

I cried and use to tear myself up inside asking the angels to help me to give me strength. I was always given a gruelling on why I divorced him and that I wasn't telling the truth this put a strain on my relationship with the girls especially Katie she got so angry with herself and Claire-Louise so she ended moving out to live with him.

This upset me a great deal but the angels said to me "let her go she has her own lesson to learn she will come back" so with trepidation I let her go. So Claire and I settled again as she was the quieter one of the two girls,

Katie used to visit occasionally but seemed angry all the time and it took great control for me not to react to her anger, deep down I missed my Katie but she had changed and needed to experience life for what it was.

Then another dark day came I had just been in the shower and was drying myself when I felt a lump, immediately my heart sunk and thought "oh god here I go again" but then a voice said "it may be nothing don't go worrying needlessly go and get it checked out".

I rang the doctors to make an appointment and went to see them the next day, the doctor said he wasn't taking any chances and booked me in for a mammogram.

When I went back for the results they found that the lump had cancerous cells so I was then booked in for the operation again I had to tell the family and again I went through the trauma of all the past issues again my mind was in a whirl and I felt like I was in a bad dream I asked the angels "why me why again? I felt it was like a test for me that the angels had given me.

The family rallied round when it was time for my operation, but this time I was not so nervous I just knew what would be would be I felt calm when the family and my friends fussed and worried over me. Once again my angel came and told me I would be all right, she gave me the strength I needed.

My operation went well and I did not have to lose my breast also the good thing I didn't need the chemotherapy I just had to have the radiotherapy which was gruelling in itself as it made me very tired, my skin was itchy and tender also I felt sick with headaches but I persevered and carried on regardless knowing that my angels were with me urging me on and giving me the strength when I felt it ebbing away.

While I had been ill Katie had realised that I wasn't to blame even though she remained living with her father she started to see for herself why I divorced her father as he did to her what he did to me stealing money from her purse,

Not paying the bills being nasty then disappearing for days on end, she was studying hard at university also she had a part-time job as a fitness trainer and worked at night in a nightclub to be able to earn money.

Claire was also studying hard at school but she had learning difficulties and found homework and studying hard even though I helped her all I could she was a very proud girl who would not let anything phase her even though she got very frustrated at times.

I had been dating for some time a guy called Andy I thought he was "the one" for me I started to trust him and he made me smile but I soon found out that he was selfish when things didn't go his way he would "finish it" he would not commit and he made me feel guilty my emotions were all over the place

But again my angels never left my side when I was feeling lost or lonely I spoke to my angels who gave me the confidence to carry on then I started to feel calm again and life began to be good to me once more.

Katie did not like Andy and used to say to me "you can do so much better mum what you need to do is go on the internet" I said to her "I am not very good with computers and I wouldn't know how to start" so one particular night when she had come home for her tea she said she was going to make a profile of me and put it on the net I just laughed it off and said "who would be interested in little old me"! Later that night we sat down together and she typed in all my interests and put a nice picture of me on too she said "mum trust me you **will** meet someone".

I was sceptical but that night the angels came to me in a dream and I saw myself talking to a screen and was laughing so much, I felt so happy when I woke up that morning was it a message that I had received that night? I pondered over it while I brushed my teeth and combed my hair the thought wouldn't leave my head even when I went to work it was in my mind.

I decided that I would have to look and kill this curiosity. When I got home I resisted the urge to switch the computer on so I tackled the house chores and made tea I asked Claire whether she had a good day at school and whether she had also heard from Katie that day which she said she had, that pleased me as I knew Katie was working through her anger with her sister and me, once again the Angels were helping me with my precious family.

Later that night I decided to just take a little look on the computer and I had a shock! I had so many e-mails too numerous to mention so I filtered through them I must admit I felt surprised but it helped my ego enormously I decided to wait to reply to them and let Katie have a look too as she was staying for the weekend.

When Katie came to the house, I showed her and she laughed and said "what did I tell you mum"! We both looked through the messages and I replied to some of them but one particular one seemed to attract me his name was Steve.

This was the start of many weekends that Kathryn used to stay finally I was getting my daughter back but she needed to want to come home and her loyalties were still divided with her father and me, so I didn't push her I just asked the angels to guide her to do the right thing I knew they were working with her helping her and giving her strength to work things through in her own head.

I just had to trust the angels as this was another road I had to walk down as well.

Angels and Essential Oils

There are various tools that we can use for attracting angelic help

But one of the most potent tools is a beautiful fragrance especially in the form of essential oils.

These oils are well known for mood enhancing, mind alterations.

It is a well-known fact that an interest in aromatherapy has seen a significant growth and also in the emotional well being it promotes.

Our ancestors were well aware of the etheric qualities of essential oils as they were widely used by priests and priestesses of virtually all religions.

They used to use fragrant oils to attract spirits, goddesses, and gods, to banish evil spirits and to purify places and people.

They also anointed themselves with sacred scents in order to facilitate divine communication.

We now know that oils and herbs were used as far back as early man

So it is through the work of Gattfose, Valnet and Maury that Aromatherapy is popular and accessible as it is today.

We are now experiencing a revival of interest in many ancient arts, which place such great importance on touch these include aromatherapy, reflexology and shiatsu all distinctive natural therapies, which have a specific role to play in alternative health- care.

The use of fragrance is a very powerful tool for drawing angelic beings close to you. Aromas open up and heighten our consciousness making us more receptive to the heavenly hosts. Essential oils because of their purity are particularly suitable for creating the vibration of love, which is ideal for attracting angels.

Essential oils are highly concentrated, naturally occurring exquisite aromatic substances produced by many different plants.

The essential oils are distilled from certain species of plants some derived from flower petals, others from fruits, seeds, stems, barks twigs roots, trees, resins or grasses

Our fragrance receptors are located in the oldest part of our brain, which is intuitive and not governed by our logical mind.

Essential oils are precious, highly concentrated fragrant substances.

Store them in a cool dark place and avoid evaporation by making sure the lids are always tightly closed.

Aroma therapist's use a wide variety of carrier or base oils to which the essential oil is added, there are quite a few carrier/ base oils which can be used neat on the skin and are also used as a general oil for massage, bath or perfume

Sweet almond, light coconut, also apricot kernel, grape seed, and safflower, wheatgerm, jojoba, avocado, sunflower, and evening primrose.

The ones easy to obtain are sweet almond oil, sunflower, and safflower

Sweet almond is used in India to heighten intellectual ability.

When choosing base oil you should always try to buy organic or the one that appears the most pure,

Pure essential oils are highly concentrated and extra care should be treated with caution here is a list of guidelines that should be observed when using essential oils.

- Do not take essential oils orally
- Never use an undiluted essential oil directly on the skin
- Keep out of reach of children and pets and any one with special needs
- Be very cautious of using essential oils on children always seek advice
- If you are pregnant, suffer from epilepsy, high/low blood pressure or any other specific conditions please seek medical advice before using essential oils.
- Keep away from the eye area
- Care must be taken with certain oils especially citrus oils
- When adding essential oils to bath water,

Dilute it first in a small amount of carrier/base oils.

Certain oils may cause sensitivity or adverse reactions in some individuals, discontinue use immediately if this occurs

Do not drive or use any machinery immediately following a relaxation treatment especially after using soporific oils

Keep products away from polished surfaces, plastic and naked flames or any other source of ignition.

There are many different ways of using essential oils for your body, mind and spirit.

The quantities recommended may seem tiny and sometimes the aroma may be barely perceptible but the aroma and the effect are in spite of this

One of the most common ways employed by Aromatherapist's is by massage with essential oils this relaxes the physical body, reliving stress, and tension.

The fragrance works directly on the deepest levels of emotions while the skin absorbs the therapeutic elements of the oils it is also wise to do a skin test for Twenty four hours prior to using essential oils especially if you have allergies to perfumes or cosmetics

Bathing with essential oils is ancient methods of purification it stirs the senses and brings attunements to subtle energies always agitate the water when adding the oils remember to shut the bathroom door to stop the therapeutic vapours escaping! Soak in the bath for at least fifteen minutes inhaling deeply and relaxing.

There are some essential oils that can be used for inhalation as a vapour.

How to use this method is pour hot water into a large bowl then add two drops of the chosen essential oil then place your face over the steam (about ten inches away) from the bowl and cover your head and bowl with a towel inhale deeply through your nose for a couple of minutes and close your eyes. Always check first before you do this with any type of oil that you are not allergic and sensitive.

Always check on the bottle of oil that it is suitable for inhalation first DO NOT OVERDOSE AS THIS COULD HAVE ADVERSE EFFECTS.

Diffusers are designed to heat the essential oil and release the aroma of the oil into the atmosphere some of the vessels are made of pottery but water bowls, candles and even radiators can also serve the same purpose.

Pottery ones can be heated by battery, candles or electric always use water with the oil never use the oil on its own.

You can now buy candles that have got the essential oils already enthused through them but if you haven't you can first light a candle then allow it to burn until the centre of the wax has melted, blow it out then add 2 drops of essential oil onto the melted wax then relight the candle.

You can purchase special rings that fit over the light bulb (table or bedside) the rings are hollow and you add the oil to the ring before you switch on the light up to 5 drops is efficient for it to take effect.

This is one of the most heavenly ways we can purify and sanctify your sacred place add five drops of essential oil to a fifty ml glass atomizer bottle filled with water shake the bottle vigorously each time you spray to mix the water and oil spray high into the air but avoid polished wood surfaces and delicate fabrics.

If you are lucky enough to have an open fire and you burn logs before you add the logs add a few drops of essential oils to the wood and leave it to soak in for about 5 minutes before adding to the fire

If you only have radiators here is another quick way to make the room smell heavenly put a few drops of essential oil onto a cotton wool ball and place it on the radiator if you have a diffuser that hangs from a radiator fill with water and add the oil to the water.

If you have silk, dried, paper flowers in a pot or vase to give them a heavenly perfume is to add a few drops of essential oils to them, some of the oils are clear and others have strong colours so choose oil that will not damage the colour of your flowers.

Essential oils can gently scent many objects in a room and the fragrance from the items will pervade the atmosphere in the room and can introduce a wonderful healing ambience to the room such as pillows, clothing, bed linen and handkerchiefs can all be scented.

A few drops of oil sprinkled onto your pillow can be especially nice if especially you wish to invoke angelic dreams/connections with the angels or it can help in a therapeutic meditation to entice the angels into the room.

Some oils can stain so use a cotton ball with the oil on it place it between the pillow and pillowcase use this method too with cushions.

A few drops of essential oils inside your sleeve so that you can breathe in the aroma when required also it is nice when you are meditating as the angels will come nearer as they love the aroma of essential oils.

You can make your own perfumed cream by adding a few drops of essential oils to a base cream (perfume free) keep it sealed when not in use as the oil can evaporate

Flower waters can be used to consecrate and cleanse magical spaces prior to ritual or meditation they can also be used to anoint sacred objects and candles and they are also an old favourite in skin care

Dilute the essential oil following the same recipe as bath or massage use as a perfume or for protection, apply to sacred objects such as candles or crystals.

It is a well-known fact that certain problems respond well to a number of essential oils

Essential oils are complex on average; an essential oil contains over 100 components

As you look at the list of oils it is possible to use a pendulum and dowse to see which oil is the most appropriate for you and your currant life situation.

When you use oils for meditation, divination or dream work always use the same oil or blend of oils as this quickly signals your subconscious mind that you are shifting frequencies there are certain oils that can invoke certain angels

To open the heart chakra also attracts the angels to healing and regeneration and renewal

Carnation* chamomile* clove* juniper* lavender* lemon* mimosa* neroli* palmerosa* piminto berry* pine* rose* Otto* sandalwood* spearmint* thyme

MEDITATION-ARCHANGEL TZAPHKIEL

To open the third eye and crown chakra invites the angel of meditation, reflection and soul searching

Clary sage* frankincense* lavender* linden blossom* sweet fennel* violet leaf

SPIRITUAL WISDOM-ARCHANGEL ZADKIEL

To open the higher chakra summon the presence of the angels of divine spiritual wisdom, knowledge, and divine understanding

Benzoin* carrot seed* chamomile* clary sage* cypress* frankincense* linden blossom* myrrh* rosemary* rosewood* sage* sandalwood

VISIONS-ARCHANGEL RAZIEL

To clear the third eye and centre chakra to quickly summon the angels of spiritual visions, prophecy and revelations

Bay* cinnamon* jasmine* lemon* verbena* mimosa* narcissus* neroli* sa ge*

ANGELIC DREAMS-ARCHANGEL GABRIEL

There are some high vibration oils that can summon the angels of destiny to send your consciousness souring while you sleep

Angelica seed* anise star* basil* coriander* dill seed* elemi* l emon verbena* Ravensara* rose otto* spearmint

ANGELIC COMMUNICATION-ARCHANGEL HANIEL

To form lasting bonds of angelic inspiration and to enhance all your communication with the angelic realm purifies the throat chakra

Carnation* grapefruit* lemon* orange* neroli* tangerine

INNER CHILD—ARCHANGEL CHAMUEL

These oils summon to our side the angels that help us resolve, heal and strengthen all our relationship these angels help us to reconnect with our inner child to bring about deep healing and comfort

Benzoin* chamomile* geranium* hyacinth* mandarin*

TRANSITION-ARCHANGEL METATRON

Throughout time people have burned incense around those who are making transition from life to death it was believed beautiful aromas would attract the angels and the smoke from burning incense or sacred herbs would carry the soul to the heavenly realms

Cedar wood* chamomile roman* jasmine* juniper* lavender* mandarin* patchouli* vetivert

FOCUS AND INTENT-ARCHANGEL JOPHIEL

To focus your intent restores mental clarity give self-confidence, self esteem

Grapefruit* jasmine* lemon* lime* cubeca* orange* ylang-ylang* tea tree

COURAGE AND INNER PEACE-ARCHANGEL URIEL

For personal courage strength and stamina to help restore inner peace soul harmony

Hyacinth* Melissa* petit grain* rose otto* sandalwood* yarrow* sweet marjoram

BANISHING NEGATIVITY AND PROTECTION-ARCHANGEL MICHAEL

For protection security empowerment overcoming obstacles and releasing fear dispel anxiety phobias and apprehension

Bergomot* camphor* eucalyptus* peppermint* oakmoss* spikenard* vale rian* yarrow* ylang ylang* lime* frankincense* anise star*

As you will notice the essential oils can be used for many things not just for healing and relaxing or massage these wonderful aromas have been around for centuries and no doubt will be around long time centuries on.

Changes

Kathryn came to stay more and more frequently but always returned back to her fathers flat and I used to spend a many a night talking and laughing with Steve,

Then one night he told me something that upset me greatly he told me that he was married even though his marriage was on the rocks for many years he said he only stayed because of his young daughter, I was taken aback and switched the computer off! I couldn't understand why I felt so betrayed as we were only talking but the sadness I felt made me cry, had I fallen for him? But it was too late as he was already married.

A few weeks went by and I seemed to recover and just put it down to experience then again I fell under Andy's spell he wanted and missed me (so he said) so my life took on the usual routine going to work seeing Andy and spending time with my girls.

It was still a struggle trying to make ends meet as I never had any help (money wise) from their father he had the cheek to say that I should pay him for Kathryn's upkeep! even though she was at collage and was 16 so I did not have any money what so ever for her and I still had to bring Claire-Louise up too!

I always made sure both girls had some kind of money to go out with why should they suffer because their father would not provide, this made me more determined to make sure that they would not suffer anymore even if it was to my cost.

This all took a toile on my health and I began to suffer then one day I had a complete breakdown, Andy had been messing me around again and decided he did not want me anymore,

My ex husband and his family were being nasty also lying and being sarcastic and causing trouble demanding things that I did not need to door hear even my own mother and brother really did not want to know either, in my mothers eyes I had made my bed now I just had to lie in it.

I was found about 6am in the morning wondering the streets in my nightie luckily it was my friend Julie's son who was doing his early morning paper round that came to my rescue.

Julie told me that her son had rung her and she came to collect me she bundled me into the car and sent for the doctor but I did not know anything of this as my brain and my body had a complete breakdown. I was in a deep dark place.

While all this was going on all I can remember is being in a thick fog like thick green pea soup, but I could see people around me but couldn't speak to anyone because this fog hung round my neck like a very heavy chain.

I was screaming inside and was frightened of sleeping apparently I used to get up in the middle of the night and used to wander around all I wanted was my dad, this frightened all the family who blamed it all on Andy but it was not true. In fact it was the past that had caught up with me and all the events that had caused it.

I was sectioned and had to be looked after for a few months and slowly the veil started to lift and I started to find my voice the chain was loosening around my neck I found out that it was all the pressure and the arguments and how I was treated by my family and ex husband that it was only a small thing that tipped me over the edge.

My angels never left my side while I was like this they did not try to communicate but I felt them comforting me it is if they knew I had to heal.

With professional help I started to put all the pieces of my life back together and I started to feel stronger my angels were urging me pushing me forward once again. My sleeping pattern started to get better and I was not afraid to go to sleep in fact I started to sleep longer and longer! It was if my body and brain needed to rest and recharge.

While I was in this state of "limbo" the family were blaming each other and my ex-husband took great delight in saying that I was "mad" he came into my home and tried to take it over but this is when I had the biggest surprise of my life, my mums husband decided that I needed the help.

He talked to the girls and made sure their father did not have access to the house he put a new lock on the front door and packed the dog and Claire to their house!

This made me see him in a different light . . . he did have a heart after all!

As the days got easier I started to work again and I started to study again, I went back to the church after a long time away and was greeted with warmth and compassion.

At this time my thoughts of Steve came back I wondered what he was doing and whether he was still married I decided to put on the computer and see if I had a message from him, but when I looked I hadn't so I thought oh well its not meant to be.

The days started to roll on in the usual pattern again and I started to feel better, healthier and set about decorating the house with gusto! Claire and I had fun choosing colours for the rooms and furnishings too it was if I needed to de clutter to make everything fresh and new! Money was still very tight but we managed to get through it.

Then one day I was out shopping and I bumped into Andy he was on his own and my heart did a flip and I started to get butterflies I knew I was still deeply attracted to him, he invited me for a coffee and a chat, I knew I shouldn't have done but my heart was leading my head everything what people had warned me about him went out of the window,

So like a lamb to slaughter I went and fell under his spell again I listened to the sugar coated words he gave me and I started to believe him so I decided to give him another chance needless to say that night I ended up staying over at his home.

At first our relationship was going well he seemed to be in love with me we went away for weekends and he even took me abroad we had a lovely two weeks away in Turkey things started to settle into a lovely routine.

The trouble was the girls did not like it and used to tell me so! But I told them it was my life and I was happy.

I always made sure that I had time for them I even started to get closer to Andy's daughter too and she used to come and stay over with me

Andy said he was so grateful because he started to get close to his daughter and they used to talk again and that it was thanks to me,

She just needed a mother and a father to listen to her and I was the next best thing. I also got on very well with his mum and dad too they told me that they wished that Andy would settle down with me as I was so good for him I just used to smile and say "well he may do one day".

Then true to form Andy did it again! He told me he could not commit and did not want a serious relationship he just wanted to have fun!

So I was promptly dumped once more the only difference his daughter and her mother even his parents were disgusted with him even his father came to see me, he said he was disgusted that his son had been a bastard to me and he was ashamed of him. Needless to say I was stunned at their loyalty and respect to me!

Andy idolized his father and mother, so his family would not interfere because they said he was a grown man and should know better, they also told me I would always be welcomed in there house this made me feel better.

The girls were livid and my family too they were worried that I may go "funny" again but I assured them I wouldn't even though I cried my eyes out when I was alone and in bed and I thought my heart was going to break as it was hurting so badly but I managed to get through each day and the tears started to ebb away,

I asked my angels to help me and give me the strength I needed and the courage to carry on as sometimes I felt so alone even though I had my girls and family I still felt lost, alone and unloved.

My studying was good and I threw myself into my work with relish this distracted me and kept me going I knew it was the angels pushing me as the thirst to learn was still there.

I had met a couple of friends who were in the same boat as me (single) so we decided to go out every weekend even if it was just to each others house and I started to look forward to this. My courage and strength seemed to grow and I started to laugh again much to the joy of the girls.

Then one night I started to surf the internet again and the thoughts of Steve popped into my head so I decided to send him an e.mail, I thought I would keep it light and ask how he was after all it had been a few months.

Crystal Children

Crystal children began arriving from the late 1990's early 2000. Many of the Indigos are now making the transition from Indigo to Crystal. In this transition stage they become more aware of their "Christ" consciousness.

The terms, "Indigo" and "Crystal" were given to two generations of children, because they most accurately describe their aura colours and energy patterns. Indigo Children have a lot of indigo blue in their auras. This is the colour of the "third eye chakra," which is an energy centre inside the head located between the two eyebrows. This chakra regulates clairvoyance, or the ability to see energy, visions, and spirits.

The Children of Crystal Vibration, or the Crystal Children, are considered to be the children of the Indigos. The Indigos had the task of changing everything to open the doors for the Crystal Children

Crystals instinctively channel healing energy.

Their crystal nature enables them to pick up energy and aura colours from the people around them. They are acutely sensitive and are even more likely to become healers and light workers than indigos, but need space to themselves and a lot of care.

Many crystal children are born autistic or die in infancy because they are so remarkably sensitive. It has been suggested that the indigos are here to transform the world to one in which the crystal children can survive and do their work.

Generally Crystal children are very connected, communicative and highly sensitive individuals.

They are extremely kind to others and often display a care for the behavior of others around them as though it were a personal experience showing their connectedness to ALL in a group conscious way.

The Crystal Children have opalescent auras, with beautiful multi- colours in pastel hues. This generation also shows a fascination for crystals and rocks,

At first, Crystal Children will tend to gather in groups where they can hold space for each other and grow together, supporting each other energetically.

They will do this all by themselves, so parents of Crystal children will not need not worry about finding the best environment for them Children of Crystal Vibration have sensitivity beyond your comprehension. They will be inside your head, knowing not only what is in your thoughts, but also what is in your heart.

At first the Crystal Children will feel like they must endure this sensitivity as a burden. The crystal colour endows the personality with the ability to channel healing energy. When a soul makes the choice to carry the crystal vibration, the personality will be drawn to the healing arts. The strength but also the major challenge for this aura colour is its permeability to other energies.

Thus, the aura is often influenced by other colours and the person will take on some of the colour of others around him or her. It is difficult, therefore, for crystals to truly distinguish between their own energy and that of others.

Their natural reaction is to retreat and they may carry a lot of fear, especially as children.

The Crystal children have similar attributes as the Indigos, yet they are more subtle and powerful than even the Indigos that preceded them.

The Indigo children have opened the door.

The Crystal Children are waiting in the wings. Is humanity ready for the next stage of evolution?

Well that will be up to us to see.

The first thing most people notice about Crystal Children is their eyes, large, penetrating, and wise beyond their years. Their eyes lock on and hypnotize you, while you realize your soul is being laid bare for the child to see. Perhaps you've noticed this special new "breed" of children rapidly populating our planet. They are happy, delightful and forgiving.

This generation of new light workers, roughly ages 0 through 7, are like no previous generation. Ideal in many ways, they are the pointers for where humanity is headed . . . and it's a good direction! It's true that the Crystal Children are different from other generations.

But why do we need to pathologize these differences? If the children are successfully communicating at home, and the parent's aren't reporting any problems . . . then why try to make a problem? The diagnostic criterion for autism is quite clear. It states that the autistic person lives in his or her own world, and is disconnected from other people. The autistic person doesn't talk because of an indifference to communicating with others.

Crystal Children are quite the opposite. They are among the most connected, communicative, caring and cuddly of any generation.

They are also quite philosophical and spiritually gifted. And they display an unprecedented level of kindness and sensitivity to this world. Crystal Children spontaneously hug and care for people in need.

The Rainbow children are the newest children to arrive and again they have incarnated at this time to become the way showers into 5th dimensional consciousness.

Rainbow children have more characteristics the Rainbow children are generally born in the year 2000 above the few Rainbow children that are here today are born from the early crystal scouts that were born in the 1980's. A rainbow child has even more depth than a crystal child.

If there was ever a bright ray of hope that the world will ascend instead of fall deeper into despair . . . it's the newest generation, the rainbow children. These children represent the wave of the future.

All children are psychic and sensitive to some degree. We are all born with intuitive abilities and have them, many just need to learn how to use them again and release any fears. On the other hand, those with heightened and developed psychic abilities and sensitivity can cause feelings of isolation and other issues, especially in childhood and throughout adulthood

These children who shall come of age in the next century bring a special gift to the world—a level of love and remembrance and knowing not heretofore possible.

Listen to your children when they wish to share their dream time experiencing. Contrary to popular opinion, dreams are very important. This is the time when the soul can communicate directly with the personality without the intervention of the ego. Dreams bring the messages of the soul and are relayed through symbols rather than words.

These children are coming forth into this world as it is written that they must at this time. It is that they carry to you remembering of that, which is, that which truth is,

That which is the essence of being, also in the reality of the One.

It is that these beings that come to you in this way are emissaries' to the ancient ways They bring to you a reality that to you seems to be one which is new. It is that this reality is of the Beginning. It is that these children carry the vibration that brings into harmony your world and the One.

These children are highly intuitive. They see all that is, and perceive all at once. They do not think within their mental structuring in linear form, but rather holographic ally.

This type of thinking brings high intelligence. Their perceptive abilities are utilizing once dormant areas of brain matter that is coming alive with the genetic changes that are occurring at this time.

Disappointments

The days seemed to roll on and the routine started again, Katie was starting to stay over longer and longer but she felt guilty about her dad and was still torn I didn't pressurise her; I just waited patiently and listened to her moans and groans.

I hadn't seen Andy for a few weeks and I was slowly getting better I didn't cry as much as I did for him I had my friends and I was kept busy talking to my on-line friends too! I felt very safe and it passed the evenings.

Then one night I was scrolling through my e.mail looking but not really paying attention, I looked, then deleted, looked then deleted, then I looked startled did a double take and read the e.mail again.

It was from Steve apparently he had been posted to Italy and the internet had been down he had hoped to have heard from me but I had sent my e.mail to his old E-mail address and it was only by chance that he decided to look at his old e.mail address and found my message.

My heart did a little flip I started to feel excited. But I didn't know why after all he was still married wasn't he? It was the summer and we started chatting again He told me he was leaving his wife and moving back into the barrack block and would I like to meet? After all it wasn't that I hadn't seen him we both had a camera connected to our computers!

So we decided to meet in London at the weekend, as I stood on the train station waiting for the train to arrive I had butterflies what if he wasn't there? What if he didn't like me? What if I didn't like him? Oh god my head was in a spin I was like a little schoolgirl nervous excited but scared too!

I boarded the train and flipped through a magazine that I had bought and my mobile went off it was Steve telling me that he was waiting for me. A flood of relief swept over me . . . At least he had turned up I told him that I was half way and would see him soon.

When the train pulled into the station I picked up my bags and then made my way out as I was walking towards the entrance it was then I saw him!

He was leaning against a wall with the most gorgeous smile he was casually dressed in a tee shirt and jeans but looked smart I waved and almost ran into his arms he gave me a little kiss and we decided to go for a coffee,

We chatted and chatted for hours it was like being with a very old friend he knew everything about me and vice versa I looked at his face and then I knew that this was the man for me but something kept niggling at me in the back of my head.

When we got to the hotel we got changed for dinner and it was then over dinner I asked about his wife, he said that he didn't love her and they argued all the time and she spent money like it was out of fashion, he was dreadfully unhappy and was going to leave her years ago but then she announced she was pregnant with his daughter he even questioned that but he said he accepted his daughter as his own.

So he stayed hoping that it would have been better with a child, he loved his daughter dearly and that was the only thing keeping him there he realised when he was in Italy that his marriage was over for him so he waited until he got back from Italy to leave her and also that his daughter didn't deserve to live in a volatile environment with arguing and shouting all the time and he had sought various advice from his fellow workers who had been in the same boat,

They all said it was better if he did it when his daughter was young rather to wait till she got older. I agreed as I had made that mistake myself and I was reaping Katie's anger for it

He had already started to ask about a room in the barracks so he had already made his mind up . . . we chatted about what he should do and how to go about it, I said I would stay as his friend even though my feelings were a little more which I didn't tell him but also the age difference was niggling at me too . . .

He was ten years younger than me and that bothered me as I felt I was copying my mother's life and that is what I tried desperately not to do,

We had a lovely weekend Steve took me to all the sights and we had a nice meal out we also went to the park and laid on the grass just looking up at the sky watching the clouds and making shapes out of them like a couple of teenagers! We ate when we were hungry and drank when we wanted to,

Then Steve took me back to the train station to catch my train and I was holding back the tears, in my mind I was thinking I am never going to see this guy again and he is just lovely so genuine and caring and it was breaking my heart.

As I walked away I daren't look back and the tears started to roll down my face I didn't care if anyone saw me I just let them go like a rippling stream in full flow.

As I seated myself in a quiet corner of the train my phone went and it was a text message from Steve saying he wanted to see me again and missed me already unbeknown to me he too had tears and had the same feelings for me.

When I arrived home I was still feeling a little out of sorts with myself so I made a cup of tea and decided to have a nice long soak while I was having a soak in the bath I thought about the past events my head was telling me one thing but my heart was saying something else. I had never been in a situation like this and did I want to be?

I was so confused I just didn't know what to do ... there still was the wife and a child and at the end of the day Steve was not free he was technically still married and that is one thing I would not do is break the golden rule of being with a married man!

I asked my angels to help me guide me and I also asked them why had they sent him to me what did I need to do? My thoughts and prayers were interrupted by the girls they were home and excited to tell me what they had been up to at the weekend also they announced that there father promised them that he would be taking them to Spain.

My heart plummeted as I knew that this was going to be another let down but that thought I kept to myself.

So the days carried on as normal the weekends the girls were thinking about what they would be taking with them to Spain and I just listened and kept my fears at bay I was still chatting to Steve via the internet on a regular basis he was my escape and I felt so safe and secure with him I used to tell him everything that I was worried about and vice versa.

Then one night as I was sleeping my phone went off it was in the middle of the night and groggily I woke up and answered the phone with a sleepy hello, on the other end of the line was Steve he shouted "I have done it"! I did a double take and sat up in bed very quickly rubbing my eyes my brain stepped up a gear and said "what the hell have you done at this time in the morning"?

He said "I have left her I have left the bitch we have been arguing all night so I have just walked out" he told me he was sat under a tree looking at the stars and he felt good and free almost euphoric "what are you going to do now"? I asked, he said he was going to sleep in the mess then get a room in the morning, go and collect his personal stuff in the day when she is at work and contact his solicitor straight away.

I just told him to stay strong and if he needed someone to talk to I was here, we talked some more then when I put the phone down my head again was in a spin I was now wide awake wondering what the hell I was going to do was I ready for this? Also I felt guilty but I had done nothing wrong in fact I tried to distance myself but the attraction was still there between us the only thing was those niggling doubts kept popping up into my head. So I decided to make myself a cup of tea and ponder on it.

I too had problems of my own I had to sell my home as I was struggling to keep up the payments on my mortgage and so with a heavy heart we moved into a rental property which was a little smaller but at least I had cleared all the debts that my ex husband had left me with, at last I started to relax a little,

The next day I had a phone call from Katie and she was in a terrible state my fears had come true as their father had let the girls down again why was I so surprised? but I was very angry to say the least, Katie explained she had gone to the travel agents to enquire why the tickets hadn't arrived as they were supposed to be going to Spain the following week and she had been giving her dad the air fare from her wages all he had to find was his own and part of Claire's fare.

When she asked the travel agent they had no record of him even booking the holiday she was mortified and embarrassed and she came rushing home to me and wiping her tears from her eyes said "my bloody father!,

Has done it again he has stolen my money"! She was so angry I tried to calm her down but one thing I didn't say was "I told you so" apparently he had met a woman called Alison who the girls hated because this woman had made it clear she did not want to entertain the girls at all in their lives, and he had been seeing this woman for quite some time,

But he also had been seeing another woman called Cynthia who the girls liked very much so no wonder he needed the money to take them out with! he soon finished it with Cynthia because Alison had plenty of money and she lived in a more influential part of the city, this annoyed Katie and Claire, but this was typical of their father.

Alison had been extremely rude to Katie she had the cheek to say to Katie "he is with me now and you have to move on" when Katie told me this my anger was reaching boiling point how could she say this for gods sake Katie was his daughter! he was spending all his time at this woman's house in fact he had moved in with her and had left Katie in the flat, he wasn't paying any bills and the debt collectors had started to knock on her door,

For six weeks Katie couldn't find him she rang her aunty, his sister and asked for her help so she was on the brink of ringing the police when her aunty had found him and told him to at least contact Katie.

When he arrived at the flat Katie vented her anger and asked for her money also asked him what the hell he was playing at! But, stood behind him was this woman who said to Katie "he is with me now get over it" Katie's anger boiled over she nearly went for her

But her dad stood in the way and held her arms down he never apologised to Katie he just turned and walked out of the door! Katie was at her wits end so she decided to follow him and she found out where he was living took the address and when the bailiffs came again she passed on the address.

She then came to me and poured her heart out to me and all she kept saying was "why mum? Why?" I told her she had done right and all I got from Katie was "I am sorry mum" that was what I needed to hear at long last I was getting my daughter back but to what cost?

She decided she wanted to take the flat over and asked her father to transfer it over but he wouldn't do it even though she tried to pay off all the bills and the rent arrears that he had accumulated. I even helped her by giving her a thousand pounds to pay the arrears off which I never got back off him according to him I owed him! Typical!

Meanwhile I was still seeing Steve we started visiting each other every other weekend he would come to see me and vice versa but his divorce was not going very well as his ex-wife was making his life miserable.

Then one terrible day my mother rang me in tears she said" Jeanie we need to talk to you" I asked "why"? And why was she crying but she just said "please come over." so I jumped into the car and set off to my mums when I got there she was sat in the lounge with her hubby he was sat with his head bowed and he looked as if as he had been crying as well I said "what's wrong"?

Mum proceeded to tell me that her hubby had six months to live that he had advanced Cancer of the lungs I just sat down in shock then my mind went into overdrive he was worried about bills and that he had to dissolve the business

So I said "not to worry I shall sort that out" but first we need to tell the rest of the family . . . then he surprised me and stood up held out his arms and said with tears in his eyes "I am so sorry for ever hurting you and not believing in you Jeanie thank you for this" I hugged him back and just said with a heavy heart "you are family".

I proceeded to contact the rest of the family and told them the news Katie took this extremely hard as she was very fond of her "uncle" (I wouldn't allow them to call him granddad) then I contacted all the relevant agencies and contacted his accountant.

That was the first of many things that I did besides taking him to the hospital for treatment also when he was admitted to the hospice I was taking mum to visit him Katie and Claire used to come with us on these visits as well.

It was as if they knew we needed to support one another, on one particular visit at the hospital I saw a thin veil around him and I thought to myself it won't be long before he crosses over.

Then the next day I took my mum shopping and we had a phone call to get to the hospital immediately as I was driving I heard a whisper in my ear "you are too late he has passed over" I held mums arm when we entered the hospital I could feel her shaking even though she visibly didn't show it, the rest of the family were there Katie, Claire, my brother we all entered the room and he was laid on the bed he looked calm and at peace all the pain that was etched in his face had disappeared.

Katie broke down and sobbed mum just kept saying "oh no oh no not again" my brother whispered to me, "we have to look after her now", I just nodded my emotions were on fast spin I just didn't know what to think or how to feel. I just felt numb.

Both my brother and I took control over the funeral and I set about dissolving his business and making sure that mum was financially comfortable she seemed to cope well with it all which surprised us. Then life seemed to calm down again.

I was working trying to make ends meet even though it was a little easier now with less bills hanging round my neck but I was having a lot of pain in my hip and again I was in the shower when

I felt a swelling just on the hip bone it was painful and tender so I thought I had bruised myself and thought "oh it will go away soon" but it didn't even after a few weeks.

So off I went to see the doctor who promptly sent me for an x ray and a scan. Again I kept this from the family as it could be nothing and why worry them unduly after all they had been through enough?

I had to wait for a week for the results if I didn't hear from the doctors then I would be in the clear. But that's not how my life was and true to form the phone rang.

The receptionist from the doctors asked whether I could come and see the doctor at my earliest convenience so I booked the appointment for the very next morning, I had an uneasy feeling because I had my angels around me a lot but I just thought that it was that my family and myself had been going through a lot of changes recently.

When I was sat in the doctors and was told the news, that the scan had showed up a mass and that they were concerned due to my past history they thought it could be cancer again my heart dipped, hit rock bottom and came back up again then the tears started to pour down my face and I just said "I cant do this again, I just cant" then all of a sudden I had a whisper in my ear "yes you can" I couldn't even remember how and when I got home from the doctors as I was in a daze but I knew I had some major decisions to make. Yet again.

Culture of Angels

There are many interpretations of types of Angels that however differ from culture to culture. Guardian Angels to protect and help guide in one belief system may also be Writing Angels in another, who write good and bad deeds down for later judgment. There are the Watchers and the Fallen, and several other distinct roles any Angel may assume depending on the associated belief system and its circumstances. The bottom line remains though; the very idea of an Angel transcends many cultural belief systems into a single collective concept.

Ancient civilizations share similar creation stories including a representative form known as the Tree of Life. Some cultures envision the Tree of Life to exhibit the flow of creation from the divine to Earth and back while others simply see it as directions for humanity to travel back to the heavens. However the Tree of Life is looked at, the fundamental principals seem to remain consistent.

The design is considered to be one of the most recognizable and the most sacred shape in geometry, believed to form the key to all of creation. Modern science uses a form of the Tree of Life throughout several disciplines, usually as a basis to demonstrate the process of evolution, classify animals and geological matter.

Genealogy utilizes the concept to trace human relatives back to their ancestors regardless of how diagrams and symbols are applied to the sciences, the Tree of Life helps humanity visualize interconnected and related elements in a tangible form. With an open mind one can see much has happened in history shrouded in mystery without logical explanations.

These occurrences are not limited to our past as they happen on a daily basis, sometimes disregarded for they may seem belittling or inconsequential at the time. Ancient Sumerian texts define the Anunnaki as "those who from heaven to Earth came" described as those who descended from the heavens, and in certain context, the fallen angels, records are filled with great details of Anunnaki having depictions as the watchers, also evident in further Biblical texts by Daniel and Jubilees.

According to the accounts, the Anunnaki were the Gods & Goddesses who met occasionally to indirectly determine the fate of mankind, if by no fault of their own. Abraham's father Terah was believed to have served the fallen angels, or the sons of the gods/goddesses, found in Psalms in reference to the Nephilim.

So digging into history as far as physical record and verbal legend allows, a great amount of astonishing literature and artefacts' are uncovered that can depict how ancient civilizations were much more technologically advanced than ever imagined. Piles of evidence are suggesting that our ancestors once communicated with beings from the sky are continuously being discovered.

It was said there was a fascinating, unique group of mystics, men and women whose chief purpose in life was to become temples of the Holy Spirit that they might receive a special revelation, and thus be the means of bringing the promised Messiah into the world.

History declares that their desire was fulfilled, that Jesus, for whose coming they made very definite and painstaking preparation, was born in the fold of their organization, these people were known as the Essene's it was also said that Mary and Joseph were Essene initiates, and that their son, with John the Baptist, his cousin, with many other biblical characters were members of the Essene communities, both in Palestine, Greece, Egypt, and many other lands.

The designation "Essene" was not popularly known, with accounts for the omission of the word in many of the popular histories and writings of the time.

The Essene attire was distinctive and unique that among the populace these mystics were known as "Brethren of the White Clothing" They were the first socialists to organize a community high above the standards of their times.

They were the first collectivists to encourage the ownership of all things in common, as mentioned in the book of Acts in our Bible, and were also the first mystic sect in all Jewish history.

Although historians differ in details, they generally agree upon the major facts concerning the Essenes. For example they agree that this pioneer group of mystics was of "dateless antiquity"

The Talmud speaks of the brotherhood as the "Holy community in Jerusalem Philo calls the mystic group "Champions of Virtue, Josephus, a member of the organization for a time, writes of Jesus as a member, and considers the Essenes to be the oldest of ascetics, The Essenes served their fellow man as minister, prophet, and physician.

They interpreted dreams, exorcised devils, and performed miracles, bringing peace to the soul, healing to the body, and guidance through the predictions which never failed.

Every adult member of the Brotherhood was assigned at the time of his initiation a definite mission in life, and this mission had to be adhered to regardless of all obstacles and temptations, even to the sacrifice of his own life.

Some chose to be healers, physicians, farmers, teachers, missionaries, carpenters, translators, scribes; others chose the feeding of flocks and rearing of bees, preparing of food, making articles of dress, or weaving.

Whatever the occupation, it had to be something constructive, not destructive. Every member worked from sunrise to sunset, and devoted the evening hours to the study of the mysteries of Nature and of revelation and the celestial Hierarchy.

The Dead Sea Scrolls were discovered in eleven caves along the northwest shore of the Dead Sea between the years 1947 and 1956 The mostly fragmented texts, are numbered according to the cave that they came out of. Some of the Dead Sea Scrolls were found in pottery jars, they have been called the greatest manuscript discovery of modern times. Prophecies by Ezekiel, Jeremiah and Daniel not found in the Bible are written in the Scrolls.

The force of light versus the forces of darkness is a prominent theme in many of the scrolls. The war scroll abounds in references to angels, all with Theo phonic names: MichaEL, GabriEL, RaphaEL, and SariEL. It is evident that the Essene community regarded them as more than simply messengers. A fragment called the "Angelic liturgy" talks about "seven sovereign princes" suggesting that angels were demigods.

One of the most puzzling questions the scrolls present is just how important were angels? Did the Jews regard angels as demigods? The Bible records that the chosen people often had a problem with belief in one God (who was all good) given them by Moses.

The Jews were under Persian control from 520 B.C. until 332 B.C. The religion of Persia was Zoroastrian. This religion suggested the possibility of two gods, one good and one evil (Ahuira Mazda and Shaitan). The theme of the forces of light versus the forces of darkness constantly occurs in Zoroastrian writings. It was a religion that believed in the existence of angels, both good and bad.

The Scrolls have some parts that are written in Hebrew, but there are many written in Aramaic. Aramaic was the common language of the Jews of Palestine for the last two centuries B.C. and of the first two centuries A.D. The discovery of the Scrolls has greatly enhanced our knowledge of these two languages.

In addition, there are a few texts that are written in Greek. The Scrolls appear to be the library of a Jewish sect. The library was hidden away in caves around the outbreak of the First Jewish Revolt (A.D. 66-70) as the Roman army advanced against the rebel Jews. The Dead Sea Scrolls were most likely written by the Essenes during the period from about 200 B.C. to 68 C.E. /A.D.

The Essenes were a strict Torah observant, Messianic, and apocalyptic, Baptist, wilderness, new covenant Jewish sect. They were led by a priest they called the "Teacher of Righteousness," who was opposed and possibly killed by the establishment priesthood in Jerusalem.

The scrolls contain previously unknown stories about biblical figures such as Enoch, Abraham, and Noah. The story of Abraham includes an explanation why God asked Abraham to sacrifice his only son Isaac. The last words of Joseph, Judah, Levi, Naphtali, and Amram (the father of Moses) are written down in the Scrolls. It is fair to say that the patriarch Enoch was as well known to the ancients as he is obscure to modern Bible readers.

Besides giving his age (365 years), the book of Genesis says of him only that he "walked with God," and afterward "he was not, because God had taken him. This exalted way of life and mysterious demise made Enoch into a figure of considerable fascination, and a cycle of legends grew up around him.

Many of the legends about Enoch were collected already in ancient times in several long anthologies. The most important such anthology, and the oldest, is known simply as The Book of Enoch, comprising over one hundred chapters.

It still survives in its entirety (although only in the Ethiopic language) and forms an important source for the thought of Judaism in the last few centuries B.C.E.

Significantly, the remnants of several almost complete copies of The Book of Enoch in Aramaic were found among the Dead Sea Scrolls, and it is clear that whoever collected the scrolls considered it a vitally important text.

All but one of the five major components of the Ethiopic anthology has turned up among the scrolls. But even more intriguing is the fact that additional, previously unknown or little-known texts about Enoch were discovered at Qumran.

In the Dead Sea text entitled the Book of Giants, the Nephilim sons of the fallen angel Shemyaza, named as 'AhyÄ and 'OhyÄ, experience dream-visions in which they visit a world-garden and see 200 trees being felled by heavenly angels. Not understanding the purpose of this they put the subject to the Nephilim council who appoint one of their number, Mahawai, to go on their behalf to consult Enoch.

Enoch explains that the 200 trees represent the 200 Watchers, while the felling of their trunks signifies their destruction in a coming conflagration and deluge. More significant, however, is the means by which Mahawai attains astral flight, for he is said to have used 'his hands like a winged eagle.'

Elsewhere in the same Enochian text Mahawai is said to have adopted the guise of a bird to make another long journey. On this occasion he narrowly escapes being burnt up by the sun's heat and is only saved after heeding the celestial voice of Enoch, who convinces him to turn back and not die prematurely—a story that has close parallels with Icarus's fatal flight too near the sun in Greek mythology

The scrolls are most commonly made of animal skins, but also papyrus and one of copper. They are written with a carbon-based ink, from right to left, using no punctuation except for an occasional paragraph indentation. In fact, in some cases, there are not even spaces between the words.

The Dead Sea Scrolls enhance our knowledge of both Judaism and Christianity. They represent a non-rabbinic form of Judaism and provide a wealth of comparative material for New Testament scholars, including many important parallels to the Jesus movement.

They show Christianity to be rooted in Judaism and have been called the evolutionary link between the two. To this day they are still finding information connected to the scrolls and ancient civilisations. In the long run the Dead Sea scrolls ask more questions than they answer. For all the questions and curiosities, however, they remain a significant discovery.

Decisions

When I eventually got home I thought what "the hell am I going to do this time"? I took myself into my room knelt in front of my angel alter and asked my angels for guidance, I knew that I had to tell the girls and the family that was without question. But what about Steve? . . . what about my studying?

For one thing I couldn't let Steve really know what was happening I had to think of something and fast.

So with a heavy heart I decided to sleep on it and come to some decisions the next day, during my slumber my dreams were lucid I felt I was sinking then flying I seemed to be crying and laughing all at the same time then I felt my angel stroke my hair and hold me as I knew I was shaking inside and couldn't stop,

The sense of calm engulfed me and I heard her whisper to me "you can do this, you will be ok"

The next morning the sun was shining and I felt that a weight had lifted even though I knew what was about to come, again I told the girls and the family they all had disbelief and anger I said "don't worry this is just another test another road I have to go down"

That night I decided to "end" my relationship with Steve After all it was unfair for me to be a burden to him who would want a sick person around them?

I was crying when I composed the e.mail I did not want him to know the real reason but unbeknown to me he was having a really bad time as his ex wife had stopped him from seeing his daughter and then I said I didn't want to see him so he felt so alone and he needed me but I hadn't the strength to cope with mine and his insecurities.

I needed all my strength to just focus on me and what I was going to go through it was selfish of me I know but it was something I just had to do.

So I started the gruelling chemo and radiotherapy but I was dreadfully unhappy and restless Steve kept in touch via e.mail we remained friends but he didn't know. we talked via the computer and sent each other messages then one night I was chatting to him and he kept asking me why I wouldn't "show" myself on camera anymore and I thought "I cant do this I need to see his face again"

Then a voice in my ear said "he will understand don't be afraid" so with apprehension I put the viewer on and he had a shock needless to say he arrived at my house the next day!

When I answered the door he was shaking from head to toe and he said "Jeanie I love you and I want to help you stop pushing me away please don't do this to me I need you to be honest with me and commit" I just fell into his arms and started to cry.

He was worried that I was seeing Andy because I let him believe it when I finished with him so I told him that I had lied and to prove it I took him to my mums home where she told him in no uncertain terms that I had been ill and had finished my relationship with him to protect him. Then he took me in his arms again and kissed me and I knew then that I had made a mistake, he was strong enough he could cope and I could lean on him.

When I had the all clear again Steve said that he couldn't do with a long distance relationship and he wanted to live with me and care for me and after all I felt that I needed a fresh start, so with discussions with Claire we decided to move to where Steve lived because in his job he couldn't up sticks like we could and it made more sense.

Steve set about finding us a place to rent and both Claire and I started to pack up our belongings with excitement. The day soon came around the removal men arrived and packed the furniture quickly then we went to the family to say our goodbyes Katie cried but she said she was ok and would see me soon, my mum said it was about time!

Both Claire and I felt that we needed a fresh start and the angels had been pushing me to do this as the dreams that I had were of metravelling and the feeling felt good for once I started to look forward to my life,

A new place with a man that loved me and he wanted my children too also my Claire was coming with me she could continue her training in hairdressing and I even had a job lined up so life was sure looking good.

Six months went by and things seemed to be going well for all of us . . . so I thought yes I had my share of homesickness and missed my family but Claire seemed to go very quiet and she took to spending hours in her room which bothered me.

I had even heard from Katie she had yet had another bad do with her father a bailiff from the council had come to the flat to give a court order for non payment of rent also she had bills coming in galore and also the one from the electric company threatening to cut her off,

I had sent her money for the bill so at least she would have heating and light but I couldn't keep paying out after all it was her fathers problem not mine!, the council also had refused to let Katie take over the flat so in fact she was becoming homeless and my mother was also worried about her as she said Katie was not looking after herself and this worried me a great deal.

Then one day I got home early from work I heard crying, It was Claire she looked terrible I asked her what was wrong she said "nothing mum" but with a bit of cajoling she eventually opened up, she just said she hated living where we were and wanted to go home.

I asked her if it was Steve she said no, she said she found it difficult to make friends and missed all her own friends I was in a quandary of what to do I was torn I loved my daughters and they had been through so much but I also loved Steve so I said to her "just leave it with me and I shall see what I could do" we hugged and I wiped her tears away all the time my stomach was churning and my mind was saying "oh god what have you done"! I decided to ask my angels for help on this one and waited for a sign.

I decided not to tell Steve until I had something concrete to do and in place so a few weeks went by when Steve came home from work and he announced to me that he had to go abroad for six months with his job. This was the sign I needed. The lease was up on the property as well so I decided to send an e.mail to my friend who had some properties to rent in Sheffield I still hadn't told Steve as I didn't want to worry him even more until I had got it all planned but unfortunately that evening while I had been in the bath, Steve had been on the computer and my E-mails had still been on and as usual the curiosity killed the cat he had to have a little look, he found the e.mail I had sent my friend and true to form he was angry he put two and two together and came up with six!

He didn't say anything to me until the next day, as usual I went to work then I had a text saying or should I say demanding that I had to come home as he needed to speak to me so I made an excuse to leave work early and went home, he was very angry he was accusing me of all sorts of things,

I was stunned, hurt then anger set in, I shouted "how dare you accuse me! I am not your ex wife! And I gave up my job, my home, and my family to be with you and even my daughter's unhappy but you're oblivious to that aren't you as long as you and your daughter are ok then its bugger the rest"!

With that I flounced up the stairs with tears in my eyes he then followed me and he put his arms around me and said "I am sorry Jeanie I jumped to conclusions"

So we then sat down and discussed what the best course of action to take after I explained to him why Claire was so unhappy and that I sometimes felt homesick myself but also that I was extremely worried about Katie so we decided to not to renew the lease on the property but that I would rent a property from my friend for six months and she even offered me a job in her cleaning firm so things were panning out. The angels had indeed answered my prayers!

Steve had a little chat to Claire that night and put her fears at rest then we told her what we were going to do, The very next day Steve was offered a married quarter through work which was a blessing as it came at just at the right time, so we started to divide the furniture some for me to take back to Sheffield the other would stay and I would come back periodically to check up on the house. Everything was falling into place in a good way thanks to my angels I just had to trust them!

When the time came for Steve to leave I drove him to the airport and we said our tearful goodbyes I knew I would miss him so much but I knew that I had to make sure both my girls were happy, so again Claire and I started to pack our belongings up and I finished my job and we set off back to Sheffield I had a lump in my throat and felt sick but I just put it down to all the stress that I was going to have sort out.

We arrived in Sheffield and moved into a very small three bedroom terraced house that had seen better days the paint work was peeling the wallpaper had faded and there were shapes of the pictures of where they used to hang and it had a musty old smell that hung in the air like fog.

My friend Stephanie had said it had been her grandmother's home and they were going to do it up but they would let me stop there for six months then they would do it up after I moved again. So with heavy heart I set about cleaning and sorting the many boxes that we had accumulated.

The décor was drab but I tried to make it cosy for Claire and myself, when I went to see mum she was ok but felt very lonely since the death of her husband.

When I explained my situation she said "that's ok Claire can come and live with me when you move back and she can stay until she is capable to have a place of her own", Claire seemed happy about the situation and she soon fell back into her old routine of seeing her friends and going out again.

While we were staying at the house strange things started to happen items were disappearing, I was having the constant smell of lilies around me things were being moved, doors being slammed for no obvious reasons, and when I was sleeping, my bed was shaken,

I asked my angel to help me and protect me and then I heard another voice it was not my angels it said "tell them I don't want it changing". I wondered what this message was.

While I was visiting my friend Barbara we chatted about it and I told her about my message she decided that one night she would stay and try to communicate, I was nervous of this so upon further investigating I asked Stephanie about her grandmother where did she die and was she happy?

She told me "she died in a care home but all her grandmother kept saying to them was that she wanted to go home and she wouldn't let us do anything in the house that's why the house looks so tired" while I was with Stephanie the smell of lilies came through again and the voice said "please don't change it".

I asked Stephanie whether her mother liked lilies and told her about my message and what had been happening in the house, she then cried and said that her Grandmothers name had been lily and that she always had lilies in her house and that she had them at her funeral too.

This explained a lot to me, so that night when I was back at the house I asked "the angels to help lily to reassure her that I wouldn't change anything and that she could rest in peace" and to also take her spirit with them to heaven where she should be, I then thanked them, after that we never had any more signs from lily again.

Twice a week I would speak to Steve via the internet and by phone he seemed to be coping with the extreme heat of the country he was in and he was going to come back for a week for rest and relaxation in a couple of months so I arranged to meet him at our house, I was excited and looking forward to seeing him again.

I had got myself into a routine I was working during the day cleaning and ironing for people, then at night I would do my readings going to the spiritual church also I would do my aromatherapy so life was treating me fairly well under the circumstances.

My old clients were glad to see me so I made enough for us to live on. One sunny morning there came a knock on my door and when I opened it, there stood Katie she was in tears looking dishevelled her hair all over the place and her eyes were bloodshot with the tears she was as white as a sheet she flung herself into my arms and cried and cried, her body wrecked with sobs, I just held her and stroked her head, I never said anything I just waited until her body stopped shaking and her sobs subsiding then I sat her down and made her a drink and just waited for her to tell me what had got her into this state, apparently she had one week to get all her stuff out of the house she had nowhere to go and her father just didn't care what happened to her, when she explained everything to me she begged me to take her in, of course I would without question after all she was my child and I wouldn't see her suffer anymore my blood was boiling at her father,

Why didn't the angels do anything? I had asked them to help Katie and they had brought her back to me so my prayer had been answered that way, why hadn't he been answerable? "Time would tell you just have to wait" I kept saying to myself.

So the next day we went up to the flat and I was absolutely disgusted what I saw, he had left her in an absolute mess! Apparently her father and his girlfriend had been and taken what they needed and left things all over the floor, papers, and bills also rubbish it just looked like a derelict or squatters house, they had even thrown Katie's belongings all over the floor; she was heartbroken and angry so we set about sorting it all out.

So I helped packed Katie's belongings up and moved her in with us it was a very tight squeeze, but one thing I said to Katie that I didn't want any arguments with Claire or myself that she would have to help around the house and go by the rules she just said "thanks mum" with tears in her eyes.

She also said "I want to go back with you mum I need a fresh start I promise I will be good and make you proud of me" I just said "I will have to speak with Steve after all it was his home too."

When I told Claire of these plans she wasn't happy because she was afraid Katie would be the same as she was before I said to Claire "just give your sister a chance she is older now and has learned her lesson".

The day came for me to see Steve again as I drove back down the motorway I was thinking about the past events I asked the angels out loud "my life is changing all the time what have you got planned for me this time? Will this be the last time I see Steve"? After all I knew I couldn't leave my girls what would I say to him? Again I asked the angels to guide me.

His friend dropped him off at the house and I had cooked a special meal I placed candles on the table and put "our" music on the mood was set to perfection, we chatted for awhile and enjoyed the meal, afterwards we cuddled up on the sofa it was like he had never been away I felt so calm and contented and at peace again.

I knew this is where I wanted to be, but also my heart was torn I loved my girls they were my life and I knew I couldn't leave them both I needed them as much as they needed me.

The next evening I plucked up the courage to talk to Steve about the situation after all he was asking me what I had been up to, I had told him what my mum had said about Claire and then I told him about Katie with no pause he said "well she shall come to live with us as there is room but she will have to pull her weight with the household chores!" I just kissed him and said "thank you" what for! He said "it's not a problem you come as a package".

Then he told me to get ready as he was taking me out for a meal. I felt euphoric as I was getting ready the weight from my shoulders lifted I then rang Katie and told her what Steve had said she started to cry and asked to speak to Steve, all she kept saying to him was "I promise I shall pull my weight I shall help I shall get a job thank you so much thank you, Steve said "whoa! Slow down don't worry I wont let you down like your dad has but that's all I ask in return."

When she came off the phone I put my arms round Steve and said "thank you" with tears in my eyes he just patted my bum and said "you come as a package remember".

While I was getting ready my mind was in a whirl, I could pack up again I would bring Katie here for a weekend and we could start to bring our belongings back down bit by bit, it will be a new start for her my only worry was that I would be leaving Claire but deep down I knew she was in safe hands with my mum.

When we arrived at the restaurant we were taken to our table which was tucked away in an intimate corner of the room Steve seemed to be on edge but for the likes of me I couldn't understand why I asked him "why are you on edge is it because of what we discussed earlier"?

He replied "no its because of this" he then promptly stood up knelt in front of me and said "will you be my wife?" and in his hands was the most beautiful diamond ring I had ever seen, I looked and looked then I cried! He said "I take that it is a yes"? I nodded I couldn't speak my heart was beating very fast my mind was in overdrive.

Steve had asked me to marry him he wanted me to be his wife he didn't just want to live with me he wanted to care for me; he loved me! While my brain was absorbing all this I still didn't speak.

He put the ring on my finger it was a perfect fit! He told me he had tried one of my rings on his little finger so he had got an idea of the size then he had it made for me while he was abroad. When I came back down to earth we had a bottle of champagne to celebrate and then we phoned our families! Needless to say they were all delighted. Yes indeed the angels had answered all my prayers things were starting to look up again.

History of Angels

Angels have been recorded in history by many different cultures throughout the world. Some scholars say that the earliest religious representation of the angels dates back to the city of Ur, in the Euphrates Valley, c. 4000-2500 b.c.e. A stele, which is a stone slab, showed a winged figure descended from one of the seven heavens to pour the water of life from an overflowing jar into the cup held by the king. Records show that in Mesopotamia, there were giant winged creatures, part human, part animal, known as griffins.

And in Egypt, Nepthys, the twin sister of the goddess Isis, is shown in paintings and reliefs enfolding the dead in her beautiful wings. Her image is found carved on the inner right-hand door of Shrine III in the tomb of Tutankhamen, The ancient Egyptians believed that each person born into the world had a supernatural double, called her ka, who was born alongside the person and stayed as a part of her life ever after. The ka was, in one sense, what we now call a guardian angel.

Without doubt, based upon archaeological evidence and other prehistoric information, there were angels long before

Christianity appeared on the religious stage. Angels are most ancient, predating even early Judaism.

The more you open your awareness to who they are and why they are here, the more you can invite their miracles of love and support into your everyday experience. You don't have to be psychically gifted to connect or communicate with angels; they are here to serve all of humanity. Just affirm your desire and open your heart to the voice of divine guidance always comes from a place of love. It will never lead you down a path of pain or chaos.

The voice of divine guidance will ask you to follow your heart and to believe in your dreams and desires. Messages from the angels are always positive, helpful, healing, and supportive.

The angels have a mission to serve and assist you along your journey. It is important to know that it is an honour for them to do so. Once you pray to God and the angels and you ask for the help you need, your job is to surrender and then affirm that you are open to receive more than you can imagine. This gives the angels permission to intervene and it affirms your worthiness to receive.

Trusting in God and believing in something greater, especially when you can't see it or touch it, is a challenge. It requires patience and determination. As you open your heart to the divine, you begin to experience these beautiful manifestations of love and naturally your faith and trust builds over time.

The truth is, your prayers are heard and answered, but not always in the way you expect.

It could be a matter of timing, where everything needs to fall into place before the answer is shown. Some people call this divine timing, which means that your prayers are being answered in God's time.

It's important to understand that you also have soul lessons to learn. You need to go through certain life experiences so you can learn valuable lessons.

Instead of having them healed immediately by God and the angels, you might need to go through the experience so you can accept its gifts and the lessons it has to teach you. This is important to understand so you can keep the faith and truly believe that you have spiritual helpers assisting you along the journey.

Everyone wants to feel safe and protected, especially in a world where bad things happen and life can be unpredictable. God and the angels want you to feel safe because fear can immobilize you. It can hold you back from living your life to the fullest. Open your heart and ask for protection for you and your loved ones, and learn how you can move into the unknown with more peace, trust, and adventure.

Being in relationships with others is part of the divine plan. God gifted you with family, friends, co-workers, and lovers so you could experience many different expressions of love. God sent you some relationships to help you grow in love, others to teach you about love, and some so you could let go in love.

God knew that some relationships would be joyful and easy and others would be challenging and heartbreaking. He sent the angels to assist you in both good times and bad.

Some people may be more sensitive to what they feel; their intuition speaks to them through sensations in their body. Others may be more sensitive to what they hear, and their intuition speaks to them through their inner thoughts or ideas. Seek to discover which senses you use the most and which ones stand out more distinctly. This helps you focus on your strongest senses to receive intuitive information.

Your intuition is a direct link to the angels. As you develop your intuition, your senses heighten and you learn to trust what you hear, feel, and sense from the angels. Intuition is the instinctual knowing you get when you listen to your inner senses. Everyone is intuitive, and you can train yourself to become more attuned to your senses.

Some people may be more sensitive to what they feel; their intuition speaks to them through sensations in their body. Others may be more sensitive to what they hear, and their intuition speaks to them through their inner thoughts or ideas. Your intuition is a direct link to the angels.

As you develop your intuition, your senses heighten and you learn to trust what you hear, feel, and sense from the angels.

Have you ever had a feeling that something was going to happen and then it did? Did you ever hear an inner voice guide you, telling you what to do, did you ever get a direct message from someone in a dream? Did you ever not trust your gut feeling and disaster followed?

Did you ever have that inner understanding and you knew you were right?

As you pay attention to your senses and you learn to interpret their messages, your intuition can become very valuable. It can direct you to the answers you are seeking.

Your intuition can communicate in two different ways. Direct intuition is literal and you know exactly what your intuition is saying to you.

Then there is indirect intuition, which is more symbolic, sometimes angelic guidance is very direct and you know exactly what they are trying to tell you, but sometimes it's symbolic and you need to ask for their help to interpret the message.

When you are confused and you have trouble interpreting the messages, ask the angels to be more literal or direct with their guidance.

New Path

After Steve had gone back to finish his duty abroad I went back to Sheffield to start packing once again! But this time I felt so much better and was eager to return.

Katie was just as excited as me and she seemed brighter in her persona she had spoken to her tutor at the university and they said it was ok for her to finish her degree long distance and that she would keep in contact via phone and e.mail so she was happy about that.

Claire started to move in with my mum so I was doing a lot of packing and unpacking the car but we all did it with happiness,

And for once I was at peace knowing my girls were being looked after by the family and of course by my beloved angels.

The day came for us to move and when I stood in the empty house I prayed and thanked lily for letting us stay in her home and I asked the angels to give us a safe and stress free journey along the motorway.

Steve had returned a week before so that he was at least there to greet the removal men with the bigger furniture.

We packed our remaining belongings in the car then drove over to my mums to say goodbye to Claire and the rest of the family this time it was not as tearful as they knew we would visit and vice versa and I felt secure in the knowledge that my Claire was safe and was happy she was home where she wanted to be.

True to form we made good progress along the motorway and arrived safe and sound Steve came out to us with a huge beaming grin on his face! He said "welcome home love" and kissed me then he took Katie in his arms and gave her a big squeeze.

The removal men had been and left by the time we had arrived so the house was upside down but before we rolled our sleeves up we all had a cup of tea and just settled ourselves I made the obligated phone call to my mother to let her know we had arrived safe and sound.

Life started to be good again I found a job fairly quickly as so did Katie and all three of us settled into a happy routine Katie and Steve were getting closer and we used to have a many a night with good banter between all of us and true to her word she helped out in the house, but Oh! When she cooked for us did Steve used to moan at her!

She used every pot and pan and utensil to cook with, so it took him half the night to wash and dry but he took it with good humour too. Katie was a good little cook and we used to say you will make someone a good wife with your culinary skills.

Steve said we should start planning the wedding so we made a date for April, I was a little reluctant as April was still sad for me as I had lost Daniel at that time but Katie said "it was time that April was made a happy time and that Daniel would want it that way after all April was spring time and that was the time of rebirth"!

How could I not disagree she was starting to tell me things that happened to her she told me "she often heard voices especially when she was down or just as she was about to go to sleep and a boy used to talk to her, I caught my own breathe! Was it Daniel? The Angel Daniel if it was she was very blessed.

I then told her that "her great Nan, her Nan had a gift of premonition and she knew that I loved my angels that she could have the same gift too" she then described the little boy and that she knew him as D it was indeed Daniel!

He was protecting his sister he had never left me so he was guiding and protecting her, one thing for sure I was going to teach Katie how to use her gift not to be afraid of it like I used to be, so when we were on our own we often sat around the table with a glass of wine talking and explaining a sometimes showing her what she had to do.

She loved helping with the arrangements for the wedding too we made all the invitations and I decided to do all the flowers myself and make the wedding cake too after all we were on a tight budget. Katie did a seating plan while all this was going on we were all working like little busy bees around the hive, so it was a hectic time indeed for all of us.

Once every three weeks we all travelled up to Sheffield to see the family I was so happy to see Claire she had settled in with my mum but my mum being a little Victorian in her ways was a little too strict with Claire and this used to annoy them both, so often I was trying to soothe the waters.

Then one particular weekend when we arrived at my mums Claire pulled me to one side and said "I can't live with Nan any more she wants me out because Uncle Clive said that it may affect her pension and her disability benefit" I was furious how he dare say that and again my mother was listening to him!,

Then my mother announced that "she wanted to move house as the house was too big for her and also Clive said it would be better if she lived nearer him" now I knew why my mum had said what she had said to Claire

When I asked mum about Claire she said "she has a father who can look after her"!

I couldn't believe what was coming out of my mothers mouth it was incredulous I nearly spluttered my drink all over her and said "I can't believe what you are saying this is your granddaughter! You know what he did to Katie? How can you do this"? All she said in a matter of fact way "I need my space" I just shook my head and said "typical mum you are unbelievable"

We helped Claire with all we could and she took a flat in a very rundown area this was all the council would offer her it was a total mess deep down I was afraid. I felt something heavy hanging around the place it felt dark and it clung like a heavy cloak around the flat.

Then the vision came in a whoosh I saw a man in a chair with a red spot around his chest I felt sick and cold something bad had happened there something very bad, I tried telling Claire not to take the place to hold out for something a bit better but she was desperate to move out as my mother had been pestering so she ignored me and took it.

With a heavy heart I helped her move in I asked my angels to keep her safe and to protect her from harm after all that is all I could do she had a house alarm fitted and new locks on the doors and we bought her some window locks so this made her feel more secure then she met the lady who lived above her who befriended Claire so I started to relax a little.

And my mother moved closer to my brother and his wife into a bungalow.

The day of the wedding came near so our thoughts and feelings turned to the last minute preparations, then one morning Steve had a phone call from his Mother, he turned white and looked at me he just said "my Father has had a massive heart attack we need to go now"

So we grabbed our coats and got into the car leaving the things as they were I scribbled a note to Katie to let her know.

As we arrived at the hospital we had just sat down with Steve's mother, hours seemed to tick by and we just drank coffee.

My mind wandered to the time that I was in hospital being operated on this time it was me sat holding the white cup, me drinking the coffee just waiting I wondered if we were being watched by his dad then suddenly my train of thought got interrupted

As the consultant came out to us and started to explain what had happened he had to put three stents into his fathers arteries and while they were doing that he also had suffered a stroke this meant that it was touch and go at the moment.

He was a very sick man we were then taken through to the intensive care unit to see him, while I was stood around the bed I heard a whisper in my ear "he will be all right its not his time" as I heard this I instinctively turned around as it seemed to have come from behind me then I realized that it was my angel telling me even though I couldn't tell the family.

I just said to Steve's dad "you will be ok you are made of strong stuff you have a wedding to go to remember"! As I looked up it was then that I saw his angel standing at his head I felt some sort of comfort at this.

Later that night when we arrived home exhausted from the days event I snuggled up to Steve and said "don't worry love your dad will come through trust me" he just looked at me with a thoughtful look and said "I do"

Something was niggling me I just didn't know why I was getting these thoughts were Steve and me meant to get married was this to stop us? Was this a message that I hadn't noticed? I just shook my head and dismissed it as a stupid idea it must be nerves that's all, after all it was my turn to support Steve and I was not going to let him down now.

Slowly but surely steve's father made slow progress but this meant they couldn't attend the wedding Steve was determined to go through with it even though I said "should we delay it?" at least until his father was well but he was determined that it should go ahead, so the day came with lots of hustling and bustling but somehow I remained very calm through it and even the sun was shining too!

My mother, brother and his wife came and brought Claire, after all she was one of my bridesmaids with Katie and Kayleigh, when they were all dressed they looked beautiful and I was so proud of them.

We only had immediate family attend at the service and toasts were made to the absent friends and family, the sun came out at the right time and it was a beautiful spring day we felt very blessed, In the evening we had friends attend, It turned out to be a very eventful night too lots of photos and drinking, dancing and eating, I was exhausted but extremely happy.

Steve got very drunk Katie and Claire were very merry it was a very funny scene to watch them all but I loved them and I was happy even though it had been marred by the past event of his fathers illness.

The next day Steve and I were going for our honeymoon to the Isle of white to the holiday home that used to be his grandmothers home,

As I said goodbye to Claire and the rest of the family Claire told me what she had found out that had happened in her flat, apparently the man who used to live there had been murdered he had been stabbed, my stomach hit the floor and shot back up! This had been my vision I had seen him! He had been a drug user and had owed money to some unsavory character that wrecked avenge on him.

This made me scared for Claire even though she reassured me that she was ok and that it had been her neighbor who had told her and the murderer had been caught and was now in jail serving a life sentence.

When I voiced these concerns to my mother she had the audacity to say "well she could have stayed with me after all I didn't throw her out"! I nearly shouted "you are unbelievable"! But I didn't I just shook my head and said "typical" she didn't hear me and carried on fussing over my brother and his wife.

I asked the angels that night to take the man away from the flat and put him at peace and to protect my girl from any harm; I wished that she could find somewhere else to live, and then I would feel more at peace with myself.

We had just arrived at the holiday home when Steve had a phone call from his ex wife, apparently Kayleigh had gone to her mother and said that I had hit her and had shouted at her during the wedding this was unbelievable I was gobsmacked!

This was something I would never have done I was dumfounded as you can imagine his ex wife was angry and threatened to take me to court and that she would also make sure that I would never teach again!

Steve told her he would discuss it with me, I was really astonished, shocked how could he think that? What was he saying to her! His loyalty should be to me I was his wife!

I was mortified and when he asked me whether I had, I said with a tremble in my voice "if you know me you shouldn't even have to ask me that" with tears in my eyes I walked away, my thoughts were in overdrive I felt betrayed humiliated, angry, disgusted all at the same time.

I went out onto the sun porch and looked out to sea tears rolling down my face this was supposed to be the happiest day of my life spending my honeymoon with the man I loved but it was turning out to be a nightmare, again my mind was in overdrive and my feelings had been hurt I felt betrayed.

I had been trying to get close with his daughter I had made her a nice bedroom and tried to be friends with her even though she was not forth coming in conversation with me when she visited, she was very much a daddies girl and I realized that it was something I had to get used to she warmed to Katie as Katie used to pay attention to her but I didn't think this child could hate me, but she did.

She was very manipulative towards Steve and he felt he had to spoil her constantly when she came this used to niggle at me as we were not flushed with money but he felt guilty because he had left her when he divorced her mother but as usual I kept my thoughts and feelings to myself but after this I couldn't not now.

When Steve found me he apologized and had been on the phone again to his ex-wife he was angry and disgusted that Kayleigh had been going back to her mother and telling her lies about us and she had been doing the same to us saying what his ex-wife had been doing so in fact she had been playing her parents against each other, when his ex wife had realized she still did not apologize to me but was in agreement that we all had to punish her.

I felt betrayed and my trust went flying out of the window, how was I going to deal with this? And to top it off it ruined my honeymoon.

That night when we were in bed Steve was sleeping, the events were rolling about in my head like marbles and I felt the tears were rolling down my face

I asked the angels to help me with this trial and get me over this hurdle I knew I couldn't cope with another disastrous relationship I asked them to help me, guide me and above all give me strength with this done I fell into a dreamless sleep.

The next morning I woke up with a heavy heart but Steve seemed refreshed and gave me a kiss and said "she isn't going to break us up Jeanie" its as if he knew what I had been thinking we discussed it further and decided to talk to Kayleigh together when she came to visit again and he would let his ex wife know what we would be doing as well.

My feelings and thoughts about her and what she had done I decided to quell to dismiss it after all she was a child and she had lessons to learn too.

The rest of the honeymoon picked up and we didn't dwell on it again we just enjoyed each others company and explored the island eating and drinking when we wanted to even the weather was kind to us as well.

When we arrived home we had news about steve's father he had made so much progress that he had been discharged from the hospital but he still had to take care for a while and he was undergoing physiotherapy as the stroke had left him with a slight limp, he had lost the use of his left hand even though it was coming back slowly, that was good news and they were looking forward to seeing us, seeing the photos and the video of the wedding ceremony.

So it was back to the routine of work and getting on with life we spoke to Kayleigh and firmly told her the rules and boundaries Steve also told her that he was married to me and that she should get used to it as also her mother had a partner and that she should respect them too, even Katie told her that she was disappointed in her which made her cry I think that disappointing Katie had more effect than us telling her off as Katie started to become a roll model to her and she started to look up to her.

Katie started dating a young man called Alex she had been seeing him for about three months when she announced that he wanted her to go and live with him and work for him in his business,

When she invited him over to meet us I was worried this man was nothing like the person that Katie would be with and again I had this feeling of uneasiness.

Steve was wary too he said "why is Katie doing this"?

Alex seemed a very nice man he was bragging a bit to us about his business but we put that down to nerves and trying to impress us then Katie told me about that he had got a child, a little boy and that his ex girlfriend was very much on the scene, I was worried, she was going to leave a damn good job and move to Essex not knowing anyone, to go and live with him and his parents in their house, I couldn't believe that she could be so rash!

I voiced my concerns to Steve and he said that we couldn't stop her but we must voice those concerns to this man I told Katie my concerns and I got "oh mum stop worrying I am not daft trust me" but I did it was him I didn't this niggling in the pit of my stomach just wouldn't go away. Or was I just being overprotective?

I decided to sleep on it and ask the angels to give me the right words and to help me with this.

So the next time he came "I said I need to talk to you as there is something I am unsure of both Steve and I are worried about this ex and the fact my daughter is a substitute for her" I asked a lot of other questions too about his parents, his job and what security my daughter would have.

Alex was very good he reassured me on a lot of things, we eventually met Alex's parents and had a good evening and we enjoyed the company.

Katie eventually moved out and moved in with Alex but every other weekend they came to stay and even brought Alex's son whom we grew very fond of. She seemed happy even though at times she vented her frustrations on me but I was her mum and I was there to listen and give advice, she worked so hard we found out that Alex's business was not doing as well as he said at first it was.

But with Katie's acumen for business she built it up again from nearly being bankrupt and it started to make a profit, a few months went by and she was now wanting desperately to have a place of her own as she felt that she wanted to be able to relax properly Katie felt that she couldn't even though Alex's parents loved her to bits it still wasn't her own home. She even befriended the ex girlfriend and they became good friends which helped the whole family life became easier for them all.

When we had time to be alone, we used to often sit in the dining room around the oak table drinking either a glass of wine or a cup of tea putting the world to right I used to relish this mother and daughter time she also used to visit Claire in her flat and they became close again which I was so pleased with, Alex started to relax around us as when they used to visit they would often arrive late and both of them would say hello and then skittle up stairs and change into there dressing gowns,

Alex used to say "I can't do this at home" he soon started to become a part of our family and I started to see him as my son. Katie also kept me informed what the family were up to in Sheffield as we didn't go up as much due to work and other commitments that we had.

We still talked about our gift and we discussed what she had seen, felt and heard, her gift was really coming to the fore and she felt compelled to read the cards and heal. We also used to meditate together and she would tell me what she would feel or hear or even see and if she didn't understand it then I would try my best to explain Katie was learning and absorbing so much like a sponge, she was very much like me she had a thirst to learn more and more.

Channeling and Guides

What is Psychic channeling?

To begin, there are two main types of channelling. The first is **Trance Channeling**, and involves basically going to sleep, relinquishing control of the body, and letting an outside entity take control, usually by speaking through the body and voice of the channeler.

Upon awakening, the channeler has no recollection whatsoever of what transpired while he was out, and for this type of channelling to be effective, a 3rd party or a tape recorder should be at hand to record the material. The material that comes out of this type of channelling is generally quite clean and elegant, as there is little ego on the part of the channeler to interfere with the information being presented.

The second and most prevalent type of channelling is **Conscious Channelling**.

With this type of channelling, the channeler remains conscious and allows expression to be processed through his body.

This is not the cleanest of ways to channel, as the material can be edited at will by the conscious channeler, but it is certainly safer than Trance Channelling, especially for beginners. Ouija boards, psychic healing, most séances, and automatic writing all utilize this type of channelling.

An important note here is that there are a lot of ways to connect with a spiritual higher plane. Anything you love doing and find that you are good at could be a form of channelling.

Who is to say that Michelangelo or Einstein even Shakespeare weren't tapping into some higher consciousness as they worked in their fields of expertise?

There are as many ways to channel as there are individuals on this earth, and we have all experienced the feeling of "drifting off" as we go about our daily lives. This is the stuff of channelling!

As with all worthwhile endeavours', channelling takes a little time and practice to produce results your goal is to put mind, body, and soul into a peaceful meditative state in order to "connect," and this does take some practice.

Start by finding a quiet area in which to relax and prepare.

This can be anywhere inside or out, but it should be the same every day.

For the first few days, just go sit in your place and try to clear the mind as much as possible. Breathe in deeply a few times, mentally pushing out all the clutter with each exhalation. As thoughts try to creep back in, focus again on your breathing to dispel them.

A little known rule for all channelling is that you have to agree to let the entity in before it will come in and start relaying information. If you are not comfortable with what you get, you can ask the entity to leave, and it must do so upon request.

You can ask for someone specific or just ask for the highest beings of light you are capable of communicating with and see what you get.

Again, if you are not comfortable with what you get, do not hesitate to ask the entity to leave. When you do connect with an entity, you will know it. You might feel a numb or tingling sensation—or you may just be dimly aware of a "presence" and get messages and images telepathically.

You will be aware of your own body and surroundings in varying degrees day-to-day. The key is learning how to get into that relaxed state and recognizing and acknowledging the input when it does come knocking.

Channelling, by its very nature, will help you to be and to live as your higher self more often because your guide is contacted through your higher self.

This means that you will automatically begin to think in higher, clearer and more loving ways as your relationship to your guide develops over time.

Who are the guides?

There are as many guides as there are people on this planet and countless more. Many of the guides making themselves available to be channelled at this time are beings of pure essence, 'Beings of Light'.

They have come from the Higher Dimensions of love and light and have come to this planet at this time to help all the peoples of the Earth to make a smooth transition into Christ Consciousness. These guides come from many different places, dimensions and planes of reality.

Some may be master teachers from the 4th and higher dimensions, some may be guides, priests and teachers from planets that are further in their spiritual development than the Earth. These guides are not here to either save you or to make predictions of a cataclysmic nature for the Earth, but they are here to encourage the qualities of love, compassion and understanding.

They are here to teach you that you create your own reality and that you may have and create all the abundance, health, love, joy and happiness that you wish.

A guide will not lie about it's origins, so if the guide answers these questions positively and you experience the guides love, or have a sense of peace and comfort, then deepen the connection by asking for a name by which you can call your guide,

You may also want to ask this guide questions like 'By which date will I be ready to make a verbal connection to you?', 'Are you the guide I will learn to channel or are you here to prepare me for another guide?' or 'What can channelling you or another High Level guide teach me?'.

Talk to your guide as if you have just met a complete stranger from another country. Ask about what your guide does, what your guide's speciality, interests is and why your guide has come to you at this time.

Your spirit guide truly loves you; they do not judge you in any way.

They have your best interests at heart and will do what they can to assist us on this present lifetime. These special spirits are your friends for life and longer!

Some people have asked me "Isn't one my relatives my guide then"? Well the best way I can answer this is that although your relatives are around to give support they aren't true spirit guides.

As lovely as our departed relatives are they would not be evolved enough to take on the role of a true spirit guide. Most spirit guides are highly evolved souls who themselves have experienced many incarnations. From what information I have received through my own guide.

Some Spirit Guides have had earthly lives at some time; some haven't. Some guides like to keep their appearance of their last incarnation as they feel happier that way.

Those that have had earth lives have long evolved and have learnt all there is to be learnt on their own journeys so they no longer need to reincarnate again. Again it is down to free will, some choose to become guides some do not.

Some guides like to keep the appearance that they had on their last incarnation, these include Native American Indians, Monks from various cultures, Nuns, Scientists, Doctors, and the list is endless.

Other types of guides haven't had an earthly existence, they are already highly evolved some of these types are so high that all you see is light, or hear a voice or sense a vibration. These types of guides are pure energy.

We have one main Spirit Guide but we also can have other guides with us as well. We will have many guides during our lifetime; they come and go as we progress along our spiritual path. Some while stay for awhile; others may only stay a short time like for instance just one day, depending on what attribute we are learning.

What is intuition?

Intuition is the instinctual knowing you get when you listen to your inner senses.

Your intuition is a direct link to the angels. As you develop your intuition, your senses heighten and you learn to trust what you hear, feel, and sense from the angels.

The more you can understand and listen to your intuition the better it can guide you.

Did you ever hear an inner voice guide you, telling you what to do? Have you ever had a feeling that something was going to happen and then it did? Did you ever get a direct message from someone in a dream or did you ever have a dream that later had significant meaning?

These are just some of the things that you can experience so as you pay attention to your senses and you learn to interpret their messages, your intuition can become very valuable. It can direct you to the answers you are seeking.

Your intuition can communicate in two different ways. Direct intuition is literal and you know exactly what your intuition is saying to you. Then there is indirect intuition, which is more symbolic, and you need to contemplate its interpretation.

Sometimes angelic guidance is very direct and you know exactly what they are trying to tell you, but sometimes it's symbolic and you need to ask for their help to interpret the message. When you are confused and you have trouble interpreting the messages, ask the angels to be more literal or direct with their guidance.

Communication from the angels flows through your psychic senses called "clair" senses. These correspond with the senses you use: seeing, feeling, hearing, knowing, tasting, and smelling.

By learning more about them you can pay attention to your senses and use them to receive clear communication from God and the angels.

Clairvoyance is clear vision. This is when you have visions, images, or symbols presented to you through your inner vision. **Clairsentience** is clear feeling. This is when you receive information as a feeling in your body.

Clairaudience is clear hearing. This is when you experience or hear clear thoughts or words' flowing through your mind and no one is physically talking to you. **Claircognizance** is clear knowing. When you have an inner knowing you feel very strong that something is true or you know beyond any doubt that you need to take action.

Clairgustance is clear taste. When you experience this you have a clear taste of something in your mouth without any explanation of why it's happening. **Clairolfactory** is clear smell. When you use this ability you can smell something even though it's not physically in your presence.

The more you learn to trust the information you receive, the more you can use its valuable information in everyday life.

By now you have learned that the number one priority in working with the angels is to ask for help. Once you do this and your request is made, you need to trust and surrender your prayer to God and the angels.

It is your natural birthright to connect with God and the angels. When the veil is lifted between heaven and earth there is no separation between you, the angels, and God. The voice of divine guidance always comes from a place of love. It will never lead you down a path of pain or chaos. The angels will always encourage you and provide you with the trust and confidence you need to follow your heart.

You are probably more used to following the guidance of your ego versus the angels.

It is only natural that this would happen because your ego makes choices and takes action based on your past memories and the feelings that were experienced from those memories once you realize your ego is controlling your thoughts and actions, you have the power to choose differently.

Recognize it and then turn your attention to the angels so they can give you guidance and direction from a higher place of love.

So get ready to hear, see, and feel their messages of divine guidance with more clarity and knowing. With this information, you can experience more peace, grace, and joy and hopefully, you will want to inspire others to do the same.

They will work with you and help you enhance your abilities to communicate in your own personal way. Continue to communicate with them and tell them what you need. They can help you raise your vibration so you can feel their messages of divine guidance and experience the clear knowing so you can take action accordingly.

You can use your intuition and your psychic abilities to hear with clarity, see with clarity, and feel with clarity. This is what I say to Katie and to all my students.

They will also help you interpret the information you receive so you can clearly understand and discern the messages.

Ask your Angels for guidance daily.

Develop your own relationship with your gifts. Learn to bring joy to them and let them bring joy to you! As you increase your own joy and love of your gifts, you create a magnetic attraction that helps bring you the resources, opportunities, synchronicities, people and places that will help your gifts to grow. Essentially, there are many interpretations of types of Angels that however differ from culture to culture.

Guardian Angels to protect and help guide in one belief system may also be Writing Angels in another there are the Watchers and the Fallen, and several other distinct roles any Angel may assume depending on the associated belief system and its circumstances. The bottom line remains though; the very idea of an Angel transcends many cultural belief systems into a single collective concept.

The idea of spirit guides is not limited to the work of mediums or Spiritualists, but can be found in many cultures and beliefs. For example the peoples of Amazonian South America believed in 'Spirit Helpers'. These 'helpers' were typically the spirits of their ancestors or animals such as the eagle and jaguar.

You may also come across the term Shaman; a shaman is a master of the shamanic abilities, journeying, ecstasy, even healing. A shaman is also one depended on by some form of a group or community. To become a Shaman you had to be 'called' to the service, often there were initiations and suffering. A ceremony which involved symbolic death and resurrection, endowed the new Shaman with a new existence, forever changing him.

During the initiation the new Shaman would meet and converse with spirits, learn how to go into trance, astral travel and be taught which spirits he could call upon in the future. Those who did not attain the full range of Shaman powers became 'medicine men'. Regarding their work, these peoples believed illness was the result of evil spirits entering inside people.

They performed an elaborate ceremony to call out the evil spirits. Only the Shaman have the power to communicate with the spirit domain, acting much like our mediums do, as a mediator and message giver.

Shamans were major figures for a tribe, often taking on many roles; teachers, poets, healers, story tellers and other functions.

A shaman must endure intense physical discipline, days in sweat lodges seeking visions, long journeys between the worlds and deep study of deities, myths, the secret language and their heritage. This is why shamanism is not a religion, but a way of life that becomes the nature of the individual.

A Dark Day

My little family were at long last settling every one was at long last happy my mother was settled in her bungalow and had made new friends Claire was happy in her job and was starting to look for somewhere else to live which I was so happy about Katie and Alex were busy with their business and saving up hard for a house of their own.

Yes everything was settled and I was at long last at peace, Steve and I were happy and still very much in love even Kayleigh started to relax around me and we were getting to know one another again.

I had a job working in a school I was teaching groups of special needs children English and I loved it! But it sure whacked me out at the end of the day,

At night I often woke up with excruciating pains in my knee I took some pain killers, massaged it with essential oils even did reiki on it, I tried to get some sleep but as the days went on it was getting worse and my knee used to swell up twice the size of my other one I couldn't even walk at times and I was often reduced to tears with the pain.

So I decided one evening when I was in tears with the pain that something had to be done. The next day I made an appointment to see the doctor

When the doctor saw my knee he said its only arthritis and gave me a prescription for stronger pain killers. Then one night when everyone was sleeping I couldn't stand the pain and just didn't now what to do with myself I hobbled slowly down the stairs I prayed, begged to my angels "please help me help me to recover please take this pain away".

Deep down I knew it was more than arthritis my head was listening to the doctor but my gut instinct and heart was telling me different even the angels had given me messages to keep pestering, the pain was not arthritis pain it felt deeper. Then I heard a familiar voice say to me "you will get the strength to get through this don't worry we are here".

Days turned to weeks and I was still in agony Steve said "this is a joke Jeanie you need to get this sorted. You are not sleeping you are now having to use your walking stick and its effecting us"! To hear this from my husband hurt but I knew he was right I had to do something.

So the next day I hobbled to the doctors again and demanded that I had further investigation this time the doctor listened to me and I was promptly sent off to the hospital to have a scan and x ray the doctor even extracted some fluid from my knee to be sent away for testing.

I felt happier knowing something was being done but I was also apprehensive of what the outcome would be. I only had to wait a week or so.

I carried on working and tried to put up with the pain and also tried to put it to the back of my mind after all there was no use worrying about it after all it may be nothing it could be just arthritis like the doctor had said I didn't say anything to the family no use in worrying them needlessly either.

A couple of weeks later while I was at work I had a phone call from the doctor he said "I would like to see you today if that is all right could you come this evening"? I replied "of course I could" and arranged with him to see him after work.

It didn't cross my mind that something was wrong until I was sat waiting in the reception area of the doctors, people were going in before me and I was the last one on the list my stomach was in knots and I felt as if I had a huge rock stuck in my throat.

My head started to spin and my thoughts were in overdrive I closed my eyes and tried to calm my frazzled nerves then I felt a presence around me and the familiar warmth flood through me I knew my angels were present around me shoring my strength up,

When I entered the doctor's surgery he asked me to sit down and then said "I have your results here jean but I am afraid it isn't good news".

My heart plunged downwards and rose again quickly and I felt the familiar panic start to begin in the pit of my stomach I took a deep breathe and said "tell me is it cancer again"? The doctor nodded and then proceeded to tell me that the x rays and scan showed that I had bone cancer in my knee and it was rare, "oh great typical" I thought it can only happen to me!

He then went on to tell me that he would book me into the best hospital that had the least waiting list but it would be a bit far to travel I replied "the distance wouldn't matter as long as I would be seen", I then plucked up the courage to ask him what had been on my mind "would I lose my leg"? "What treatments would or could I expect"?

After I left the doctors surgery with all the relevant papers and forms in my bag I started to hobble home, I passed the park and saw the children playing and couples walking their dogs then the tears started to flow I just couldn't stop by the time I arrived home my eyes were red and swollen.

I was sobbing uncontrollably my body shaking from head to toe I couldn't put the key in the lock but I eventually managed I almost fell in through the doorway in my mind was the urgency "I must tell Steve, I must ring him now".

I dialled his number with shaking hands and tried to take a deep breathe; when I heard his voice my voice cracked he kept saying "what's wrong love? Then I said "I have the results Steve it's not good"

Then I heard an intake of breathe then "oh Christ babes I am coming"!

Within ten minutes he was home he grabbed me and I sobbed and sobbed and sobbed he just continued to hold me feeding me his strength holding me and soothing me he said "we can do this together babes we will get you through this".

After I had calmed down and the initial shock had subsided a little he proceeded to ask me what the doctor had said and what was the next stage I then told him and showed him what the doctor had given me. Then I realised that I had to tell the family yet again!

The tears started to well up in my eyes and my voice started to crack Steve held me again and said "don't worry babes I shall tell the girls and the rest of the family you don't have to do anything". The relief of that left my shoulders.

So I just sat there numb in shock and trying to comprehend why me why again?

Later as I lay in my bed I asked my angels "why do I keep having trauma like this why do I have snatches of happiness why me? Please give me an answer"?

Then I had my reply "you are stronger than you think you will overcome this".

I silently cried into my pillow when I felt the familiar warmth go through my mind and my body soothing me calming me and finally blessed sleep came to me.

The next day Katie and Alex came to see me she immediately hugged me and said "oh mum I love you please fight this you can do it we are all here to help you just tell me what to do" I just said "just be there for me and help me with your strength" she nodded and hugged me again, then she said "now sit down we are going to do the tea and tidy up".

Then she gave me a bouquet of red and yellow tea roses and a little box she said "this will help you mum" as I opened the tissue paper inside was a little rose quartz angel it was beautiful she said "you can have it with you when you go into hospital" I hugged and thanked her then she started to fuss over Steve and Alex and telling everyone what to do.

Then the telephone rang it was my Claire she was worried and had cried when Steve had told her so I just reassured her that

I would be ok and that she could come and see me when I was out of the hospital we then chatted about other things.

We finished our conversation with a promise that I would keep her informed of everything that will be going on I put the phone down knowing she was feeling calmer and satisfied.

I felt exhausted and started to doze off but in the back ground I could hear the voices of Steve and Alex also Katie having a conversation I couldn't make out what they were saying as I was drifting deeper and deeper it was then I heard another voice it was my angel "continue your work what will be will be". I woke up from my slumber thinking what did she mean what will be will be?

I decided not to dwell on it after all I had other things that I needed to think about such as my job and what the consultant would say to me.

When the time came for me to attend the hospital I was surprisingly calm Steve was sat with me, holding my hand and occasionally giving it a squeeze to reassure me then I was called in to see the consultant he looked at me over the top of his glasses and said "well then lets have a look at this knee" he firmly got hold of my leg and started to press and feel around the joint humming and ahhing as he proceeded to examine my leg then he said "right I will have you in to have an exploratory operation, first lets take a little look inside before I start taking anything away I shall have you in as soon as possible please see the reception to book in", I was amazed how abrupt but efficient he was I came out feeling at least I was in good hands.

A couple of days later I was sat in a chair wrapped in a gown with nhs printed all over it, I had a paper hairnet on blue socks on my feet with a huge arrow drawn on my leg waiting to be taken into the operating theatre I certainly wasn't a fashion statement! I was still in a whirlwind it was happening so fast I couldn't get my breathe I was just travelling with the tide guided here and there everything was out of my hands and control I just went with it all feeling bewildered.

The anaesthetist came and asked me the obligatory questions which I answered my nerves were surprisingly calm after all this was something I had done so many times and I knew my angels and guides were with me and in my hand I held my little angel that Katie had given me,

The time came for me to go down to theatre I kissed and put the angel by my bed, my heart began to pound in my chest like a big base drum and I started to feel sick my thoughts began to think back what the doctor had said to me I hoped to god that the cancer hadn't gone so far that I would have to lose the whole leg I hoped that he would at least be able to save it, time would tell and I would find out later on that day I gulped the feeling down and pushed the dark thoughts to the back of my mind.

I woke up feeling very groggy and sleepy and looking into my face was the doctor he said to me holding my hand "good news jean you will have to have a new knee but you wont lose your leg so don't worry I am going to put you on chemotherapy tablets straight away and we shall book you in for the operation as soon as possible."

I just closed my eyes and thought am I dreaming did I hear and see the doctor? Then I drifted further into a dreamless sleep,

Sometime later I woke up on the ward feeling refreshed and I was starving my stomach was making the most awful growling noises when a smiling nurse came in and said "oh you are awake now!

Your husband has been calling and your children", she was chatting away to me as she was straightening my bedclothes and taking my blood pressure she then said "oh has the doctor been to see you and told you the outcome"? I replied "I think so but I wasn't sure I was dreaming."

She laughed and said "that usually happens I shall have a little look what your notes say" with that she bustled off I just lay back onto my pillows and looked up to the ceiling my leg didn't feel like my own it was numb and this huge bandage was wrapped around it and a couple of crutches were put on one side ready for me I thought here I go again can I get through this, do I want to?

Then as if on queue a whisper in my ear said "yes you can" with that I picked up the little quartz rose angel looking at it said "yes I can do this".

The family were waiting for me when Steve took me home and as usual I was greeted with are you ok? What was the outcome? What do you want us to do?

We discussed what we should do and I decided to leave my job my head was spinning and I just knew I had to think of myself now.

When I was taking the tablets my body went into shock my skin became dry and itchy and I was feeling sick all the time so the doctor gave me anti sickness tablets I slept then got up made a drink then slept again this seemed to become a pattern with me but luckily the family understood and left me to do what I needed to do,

The day of the main operation dawned I felt nervous and my heart was again pounding in my chest, in my ears, I couldn't stop shaking and the feeling of sickness returned even though it was only apprehension this time I kept saying to myself "come on Jeanie get a grip" again I was waiting beside my bed with the nhs gown, bright blue socks and the lovely blue hairnet covering my hair, I was trying to keep my mind calm by flicking through a magazine that Steve had bought me earlier he couldn't stay with me as he had to get back to work but I knew I would be seeing him later.

I was also making idle chatter with another woman on the ward just to pass the time as I knew she was feeling the same this seemed to help me as well as the woman with our impending operations.

The anaesthetist came to see me and took my blood pressure when he gave me a bombshell he said "because your blood pressure is so high we cannot put you under so we are going to give you an epidural into your spine you will be awake but we may just sedate you to keep you calm" with this news I though "oh my god no I am going to have my knee removed while I am awake"! my stomach literally plunged downwards and I felt sick.

I voiced my concerns so he said "don't worry we will sedate you and you will not see anything" this news brought fresh feelings of worry and my body shook even more, even though I was sat down I couldn't stop my knees from knocking and I couldn't even read my magazine because my hands were shaking so much I kept thinking "ok I may not see anything but I would hear things" what about that?

I just hoped that I would be knocked out enough. The time came for me to go to the theatre and the porter collected me and was cracking jokes all the way even though I was trying to laugh at his jokes I still couldn't relax the anaesthetist proceeded to talk through what he was doing and then blackness came. I briefly woke up to hear some banging of metal and a sawing sound but a kind nurse with lovely green eyes said "you are ok Jeanie just close your eyes and go back to sleep"

To which I did . . . a few hours later I was back on the ward with my leg swathed in bandages and it was resting on a couple of pillows I reached out and picked up my little angel. It was going dusk when Steve arrived with magazines and chocolates in his hands he gave me a peck on my cheek and said "how are you love, well its over and done with now at least you have still got your leg but you now have a bionic knee" with that remark I smiled.

Steve had arranged with my mum for her to come and stay to help me when he was at work as I would be too weak to do anything when I came out of hospital and I would definitely need some help the doctor said that he had managed to take away all the cancerous cells and had taken a bit more bone but he had built it up and I would be limited but at least it had been successful.

I thanked him and felt a huge weight lift off my shoulders I would be able to look forward to the future again even though I still had physiotherapy and appointments to attend but things were starting to look rosy again.

The summer was soon upon us and one thing that my hubby and I liked doing was spending time in the garden tending the plants playing with our pet dog and going to car boots this also rubbed off onto Katie and Alex and when they used to come and visit us for the weekend Katie used to say "where are we going today? I love a bargain" so we all used to pile into the car and head off to the event.

Alex and Steve invariably walked on ahead and I used to hobble behind with my walking stick Katie hanging on to my other arm, we always came back with something more often some more plants for the garden so the garden was always a riot of colour,

I often sat in the garden on my garden swing absorbing the sunshine on my body I would tend to drift letting my thoughts wonder this was always a time for reflection for me.

When I had finished my meditation I used to come back to the now feeling at peace and refreshed everything was so calm. These were good days and at long last I started to think of the future I was looking forward to seeing both my daughters settled and becoming a grandmother one day. Katie and Alex were saving up hard for their house and they had become engaged so yes I felt for once that I was being rewarded. I was not afraid to look forward again

Spiritual Care

S piritual Healing is a natural energy therapy that complements conventional medicine by treating the whole person— mind, body and spirit. Healers are thought to act as a conduit for healing energy, the benefits of which can be felt on many levels, including the physical.

Spiritual care is to devote spiritual presence attention and assistance to those who are feeling vulnerable through trauma.

The word trauma evolved from the Greek word for "wound." When people experience trauma or a disaster, they feel vulnerable.

Healing comes from people's ability to reclaim their lives; including their abilities to self-determine and make decisions. The use of language is a major contributing factor to healing. Human contact and compassion are also powerful tools to be used on a journey of healing you will notice a variety of expressions in storytelling and in how individuals refer to themselves.

Some want to be called "victims" because they want others to know of their pain, suffering, and ongoing struggle. Others quickly state that they are "survivors" because they have endured a crisis and are moving to recover their lives. So how can we respond spiritually to these people?

1st Provide immediate relief from pain and help by offering healing 2nd provide time for them to help them through the problem

3rd help them with their coping skills and/or develop new ones.

4th use whatever resources are necessary and available to meet the crisis. For example reiki/crystals

5th Assess the person's ability to function and refer the person to further assistance if necessary for further reiki treatments, crystal healing, or any other treatments that you may use.

Before you work with anyone you need to protect yourself so as I say turn on your GPS!

In other words you need to GROUND yourself you must do this if you are about to enter a situation where you will be dealing with pain, suffering and grief, it is very important for you to ground yourself. Grounding techniques can help mitigate the effects of extreme dissociative episodes where you may experience distancing from your body, your environment, or the people around you.

You need to PROTECT yourself, first you need to ask the angels for assistance after grounding yourself, send mentally a request to the higher beings of light and love that operate under the Law of One. The purpose of Spiritual Crisis Intervention is to reach out to the inner levels of a Human Being, through the assistance and support that would empower the one in distress to be able to return to normal functioning of daily life.

Then you need to SHIELD yourself there are many techniques for shielding such as putting yourself in a protective bubble, chi ball, even a tube of light

Make time for reflection also try to Spend time with nature this is good for grounding

Find a spiritual connection or community it helps if you have someone or somewhere you can relate to.

Be open to inspiration listen and hear everything around you with an open mind.

Cherish your optimism and hopes try to stay positive with everything you do

Identify what is meaningful to you and notice its place in your life basically prioritise what is in your life.

Find time to Meditate, Pray even sing!

There are various healing tools that you can use such as crystals each crystal has a certain function that can aid Aromatherapy and essential oils there are different types of oils that also help aid with healing they can also help alleviate feelings and bring immediate relieve.

Reiki hands on healing can help clear blockages and help restore the inner harmony through hands on healing.

There are many ways to restore lifestyle balance, and keeping track of and making progress

Such as physical self care, psychological self care, emotional self care, and spiritual self care, Healing also means having a greater ability to manage trauma-related emotions and having greater confidence in one's ability to cope.

So in order for us to stay healthy in everyday life it is important for us to remain in harmony with ourselves we can work on even more effectively on personal themes problems and the causes of illness, through meditations and healing "conversations" with the body, we can further intensify inner growth and healing.

So by respecting and loving our bodies and accepting ourselves as we are we do experience healing. We all have a healer within us in other words our gut feelings knows the answers and the correct healing methods for our problem we can help our inner healer by feeling and listening to it.

The Worst Year So Far

Days were starting to come and go and a routine had been established yet again I was progressing well with physiotherapy and getting stronger everyday, the summer came and most weekends we had a bbq and the family and friends would come around where we would enjoy their company and have lots of laughter, yes things were starting to get better I could relax and start to look forward to the future with my beautiful family.

Autumn started to set in Katie and Alex were busy with work also she was looking at wedding venues as they told us that they were planning to marry in the January, Steve and I told her that we would buy her the wedding dress and I would also do all the flowers so when we were together she was showing me samples of what she would like she was so happy and so excited and the conversations always turned to the wedding.

Claire-Louise was doing well in her little job and she was settled so I started to relax knowing she was doing ok and seemed happier as well. For once I started to look ahead.

Christmas was coming thick and fast and everyone was asking me for Christmas cakes it was also Katie's birthday in the November so we planned to get that out of the way before I attempted to start the Christmas festivities! They were all going to come over to stay for a long weekend to celebrate her birthday I planned to cook her favourite meal and Claire-Louise was coming as a surprise Kayleigh had made her a special birthday card too.

The day arrived and Alex and Katie came into the house I was in the kitchen and I heard lots of happy voices and the dog barking excitedly and with a rush she came into the kitchen saying "hello mummy" and gave me a hug and a kiss, It was then I took a look at her she looked very tired black lines under her eyes and she looked very pale I voiced my concerns but she shrugged it off saying "don't worry mum I have a bit of a cough and cold that's all".

I looked at her wearily and said "I hope you are resting and taking something for it" "oh mum will you stop fussing!" I shall be ok" was the reply but in the deepest pit of my stomach the familiar stirrings of worry started to unfold I just told myself that it was a motherly thing to worry when your children look so ill.

The weekend went without a hitch and everyone seemed to be enjoying themselves the meal went without a hitch and Katie opened her presents but this nagging doubt kept creeping in she just didn't look right.

After Katie's birthday all our attention turned to the Christmas festivities there were parties to attend shopping to get and lists to make . . . it was a very busy time indeed we had planned to go up to Sheffield just before Christmas to see my family and do the rounds of friends and relations.

Katie and Alex then came for a weekend as they were having Christmas with Alex's parents and the New Year she was planning to see her father and my family,

I put the Christmas decorations up and I was reminded with each bauble and tinsel of what the girls were like at Christmas I still hung there stockings on the fireplace.

Even though they were grown it still seemed the right thing to do after all it wouldn't be Christmas without them I always remembered their smiling happy faces and how they squealed with excitement of putting a mince pie and a glass of sherry out for Santa and of course a carrot for Rudolph.

I enjoyed putting the Christmas tree up and waiting to see their reaction in the morning when they came trotting and skipping down the stairs just to see their eyes go bright and wide when they saw the tree with the lights on twinkling away. I always hid a chocolate on the tree for them and they took great delight playing the game of hot and cold to find it.

This was the only time the girls ate there breakfast in a rush so they could have the chocolate bar. Yes Christmas always held special memories for me, even though I struggled with money when the girls were growing up I always tried to make it special for them.

In the middle week of December Katie and Alex came to stay and as soon as I saw her I was shocked and worried how ill she looked the pallor of her skin was grey and her eyes had lost their brightness her voice was raw and she was shivering, I immediately made her a hot drink and said to her have you seen a doctor yet? She replied "no we have had to get the orders finished"

I darted a look to Alex and said "you can't work if you are ill you have to look after yourself"! Alex said "I told her to have a couple of days off" I said "she needs more than a couple" and I just sucked in my breathe very hard and my body language told him I was not happy that my girl was still ill!

I sent her to bed and when she was settled I spoke quietly to Alex and said "promise me that you will make her go to the doctors she needs rest", while we were talking we heard the faint sounds of her coughing and spluttering, then the sinking feeling of worry started to rear its ugly head twirling my guts round and round like a washing machine.

A few hours later I went up to her with one of Steve's special hot toddies she woke groggily from her sleep and said "how long have I been asleep"? I told her not to worry about that and that she needed the rest I stroked her hot head silently and I sent some healing to her as I did this, I said "Katie please go to the doctor even if its just to make me happy if not I want you to stay here until you are better"?

She said "ok I will go to the doctors but I can't stay it's too near Christmas".

I felt a little easier when she said that and Alex had promised me he was going to either get the doctor out or make her go to see the doctor.

The mini Christmas dinner didn't go quite to plan as Katie couldn't eat and spent most of the weekend in bed even though she tried so hard to join in she was so weak. The night before they went home, I prayed to my angels pleading with them to look after her and help heal her.

I did not sleep very well I was disturbed by the racking coughing coming from her in the next room and I heard Alex get up to get her a drink I shot out of bed and asked him if she was ok he said he was getting her a drink and some paracetomol I then got back into my bed eventually I went back to sleep but it was not a restful one I was so worried and I couldn't rid myself of this feeling.

When morning arrived it was very bitterly cold the snow had been falling and it had a definite nip in the air, I told Katie to wrap up warm tugging at her scarf and coat she looked like a ghost so white and pale almost translucent my heart ached to see her like this and I felt hopeless all I wanted was to keep her safe and warm but I had to let her go which wasn't easy.

When they had gone I turned to Steve and said "I am really worried about her" with a slight sadness in his voice he said "I know babes she is ill lets hope she does go to the doctor she should have stayed here at least for today".

I rang Alex the next day to ask whether Katie had been to the doctors and he said yes she had and that she had the flu with a chest infection so she had to stay in bed, I briefly spoke to Katie and made her promise me that she would look after herself

With that I put the phone down with a sigh.

The week leading up to Christmas we had a phone call from Alex, Katie had been admitted to hospital with breathing problems, we got the directions from him and where she was in the hospital.

As I was putting my coat on I turned to Steve and said "you know I think I knew this was going to happen she just didn't look right and my instinct kept telling me . . . I was not being a fussy overprotective mother at all"! He said "I know babes don't worry lets just go and find out what they are doing for her".

We arrived an hour later to the hospital and found the ward I saw my beautiful girl laid in bed so white she nearly faded into the clinical white sheets,

I gently put my hands on her head and kissed her forehead she looked up at me her eyes so sad, so tired so drained, and I spoke softly choking back the tears that threatened to overflow and whispered "you are in the right place now hunnie try to get better" I took hold of her hand and she squeezed it and she croaked "I will try mum" with a tear dropping from the side of her eyes.

Alex kept us informed what the doctor had said during that week as it was a distance to get to the hospital everyday even though I rang everyday to find out what they were doing and how she was but the other person on the other end was always in a hurry and gave very little information and this was so infuriating at times!

But one night I had a nightmare Steve woke me up I had been crying and shouting "no don't take her"!

I lay trembling I knew what was going to happen and I didn't want to know I pleaded silently to my angels "please, please help her get well" but two days later she was taken into intensive care.

We arrived at the intensive care only to see my ex husband and his girlfriend sat there, Alex felt that he had a right to know and deep down I knew he was right so through gritted teeth I was polite to them both and kept my feelings at bay after all my baby was lying in intensive care all wired up and the hospital had told us that they had put her into a coma to give her body a rest and her lungs so the machines were actually doing the work.

We had a meeting with her doctor who explained that Katie's body was so exhausted that she couldn't fight any longer she had contracted streptococcus and pneumonia so they were bombarding her with antibiotics and they had put her into a coma to let the antibiotics do there work and she was given oxygen to breathe,

When we were taken in to see her, my legs buckled everything in my head was screaming no, no, no! I held on to Steve and was shaking head to toe we donned the gowns and washed our hands before we could touch her, this isn't happening, not to my beautiful girl, not my baby!

There she was with a tube down her throat wires all around her and the machines making noises lights blinking off and on there was a nurse at the foot of her bed who smiled and introduced herself to us and explained what the machines did.

I took hold of my girls hand and said "Katie I know you can hear me Please, please get better I need you"! With this my voice cracked and I let the tears flow . . . Steve put his arm around me and said "she is a fighter like you babes she will try".

We arrived home both with heavy hearts and I spoke to all the family and informed them what was happening even friends too, Christmas went out of the window my every waking thought were for my girl. Claire came down with my ex husbands sister to stay overnight then she later came again with her father.

I kept her informed and told her not to worry as the hospital were doing what they could for her, I knew I was just delaying the truth but I didn't want to listen to it.

Christmas came and went through a blur we just went through the motions I cooked the Christmas dinner but didn't really enjoy it we watched the films that were on the TV without really absorbing anything sadness clung to me like a disease I was struggling on the inside but trying to stay positive on the outside.

One night I couldn't sleep so rather than disturb Steve I crept down the stairs and sat huddled on the settee and I prayed and prayed and sobbed silently it was then I felt a soft hand on my head and in a whisper I heard "you have to be strong its time". I knew that it was my angel telling me what I already knew what was going to happen.

The next morning I rang my brother and my mother and said "you have to come today we need you down here", without asking he said ok and they immediately set off that day.

They arrived late in the evening and I updated them on Katie's condition,

I spoke with no emotion just as if I was just reading a script. Steve said "when she gets better we shall give her one hell of a wedding" to which everyone agreed I just nodded but kept my thoughts to myself of what I knew was to come I didn't have to wait long.

Around 7. am in the morning I received a phone call from the nurse saying that I should come to the hospital straight away. I started to shake and said with a tremble in my voice "ok I shall be there" I then shouted all the family to get up as we needed to go to the hospital

I was holding back the tears and feeling very sick my head was spinning and I kept saying to myself "be strong don't buckle just be strong"

The traffic was good to us as we made good time but we were too late. As we entered the hospital I felt something in my heart go I stumbled and started to shake Steve grabbed me and held my arm we arrived at the intensive care unit and outside the double doors was my ex husband his face was white and he was visibly shaking he had tears in his eyes when he saw me he put his arm around me and said "our baby has gone" . . .

I started to scream in my head "no, no, no, not true she can't go god can't take her

It's not fair"!

I felt my heart plummet into darkness the intense heat of the pain as it was breaking took my breathe I felt all my body my mind falling into the darkness of despair I was crying screaming and I felt I was choking from this darkness

My body was shaking and my stomach was sinking fast I felt every emotion come altogether I was on a fast spin to no where I was falling deeper and deeper into a black hole and couldn't get out.

I was brought to reality with Steve holding me and saying "oh babes come on" . . .

In fact I had screamed out in pain and had collapsed to my knees.

He had picked me up and put me on a chair and was holding my face looking at me which brought me back to the dark reality of what had happened.

I was trying to breathe but the breathe was not coming, I was dying inside I felt that a thousand knives had been stabbing my heart and soul.

Then I knew I had to see her so I stood up legs wobbling and tears streaming down my face I said "I want to see her now" the doors swung open and the nurse was waiting for me she got hold of my other arm gently, she was also crying and said "I am so sorry so sorry", she then guided me to Katie's bedside.

When I saw my beautiful girl laid without the wires without the familiar sounds of the machine keeping her alive my lips trembling my eyes were filled heavy with tears my lips trembling I held her face in my hands and let my tears flow and sobbed and sobbed with every racking breathe I didn't care who heard, who was there I was just alone with my beautiful girl who had left me.

I stroked her beautiful long blonde hair sobbing I held her hands that had turned so white that looked and felt like a china dolls so cold, I looked upon her face with her beautiful dark eyelashes that were still long thick and black that rested almost on her cheeks I laid my head on her chest and held her in my arms and sobbed and sobbed from the deepest part of my soul.

My Katie had left me but something made me look up it was then I saw a white light above her and then it faded and disappeared I knew then her soul had completely left her body when I looked around everyone was in tears then I saw my other beautiful girl and I knew then I had to be strong for her.

We both crumpled into each others arms and sobbed and sobbed time just seemed to stop for us, everything was in a daze we were like the living dead nothing could help us out of this despair.

We eventually came home trying to let things sink in Steve kept saying "how the hell did it get to this"? I was broken I was dead; dying inside I forced myself to do things I had to after all I had another daughter who was in pieces too.

I just let the tears come for days on end during the night too I wanted questions answering but the angels wouldn't give me any I was angry with everyone with God, with the angels, with the hospital, with Alex, with my ex-husband, I needed to blame I needed those questions why had she died no one dies of pneumonia not at the age of 25!

Even though I was grieving my angels never left me they were there I could feel and sense them around me but I wouldn't let them near me they were waiting in the wings ready to come on the stage in the next act of my life. They let me grieve they comforted me in my dreams. Yes they waited to heal me again.

So instead of arranging a wedding we had to think about Katie's funeral, I couldn't bring myself to do her flowers so Alex's parents arranged everything but true to form Katie's father didn't pay for anything it was down to Alex's parents and Steve and I even though her father kept saying he wanted certain things which I tried to do. we decided to have her cremated and then take her ashes back to Sheffield to take "her home" as many of her friends couldn't travel the distance from Sheffield to Essex.

The day of the funeral came I was still walking in a daze not sleeping very well crying and I felt I was in a nightmare that I couldn't wake up from.

Katie's father and his girlfriend came with his side of the family and we said a polite but very strained hello.

Katie was carried into church by Steve, Alex, John and her father; with the sound of Ave Maria in the background I noticed that the church was full Claire-Louise and Alison were flanked on either side of me as we walked behind the coffin.

My legs were buckling and I was shaking I let the tears flow I didn't care I was alone in despair in this dark pit no one could get me out or hear me screaming inside.

Later on at the wake people were coming up to me, telling me that they were so sorry these people were strangers to me but they knew my Katie or had worked with her, I listened to there stories of how they met her and what they thought of her.

They didn't have to tell me about my Katie I already knew she had been cruelly ripped away from me inside I felt like screaming at them "what the hell do you know of my daughter you have only known her a short time she was my life! Do you really know what I am going through"? But of course I didn't I just kept these thoughts in my head.

As I looked around the room I noticed that Katie's father had been quietly sitting in the corner drinking. And my heart started to sink oh god I thought why does he have to get drunk here, why doesn't he respect Katie she wouldn't have wanted this! Even his girlfriend was the same I started to feel so ashamed and embarrassed to be in their company.

When everyone had gone Alex's parents were tidying up I set about helping them I needed to occupy my mind in the other room Katie's father was still drinking he was so drunk that he was spilling drink and showing off telling his usual lies.

Even Claire-Louise was disgusted with him and said she would never talk to him again she disowned him from this day forward.

It was at this point that Steve and Alex saw my face and decided to take him and his girlfriend back to their hotel. When they went I apologised to Alex's parents and I was surprised when they said Katie warned us what he was like and we are under no allusion of what he is so don't worry.

The house seemed empty and cold even though she hadn't lived with us for a year but knowing her laughing face and her voice was not ever going to come through the door never to have a cuddle from her, or her to shout my name when they arrived. It still felt unreal and hurt like hell!

I arranged with Alex to collect Katie's belongings at a later date as I couldn't face to do it just yet even though his parents were pushing to get things sorted. I felt it was too soon my courage had been spent and I had to recoup to be able to cope with the next hurdle. That would be her memorial service in Sheffield that way all her friends and the rest of the family could come and say goodbye too.

Steve and I discussed with my family what Katie would have liked again her father did not even pay out or even offer but made enough noise or rather the girlfriend did when we didn't do what they wanted, but why should I? After all he couldn't really say anything after the way he treated my girl before!

We decided after the service we would go back to my mum's and just have tea and cakes and when Katie's father and relations went both Steve and I would take the family out to dinner and celebrate her life.

Days turned into nights and weeks into months, I eventually collected my Katie's belongings and went through them with Claire-Louise somehow we felt comforted with them we smelled her perfume on them and drank it in relishing it and savouring it clinging on to the memory of her.

I still wouldn't let my angels near me I only wanted my daughter back then I felt an urge to meditate it was then I felt her around me was I dreaming? I couldn't contact her I tried and tried but she seemed to be behind a veil, a friend of mine Penny suggested that she could try by inviting her over and she did which I was so grateful for She then told me to talk to my angels so I decided to meditate again and talk with my angels.

I felt them around me hold me and filled me with warmth I knew that they had been waiting for me to ask them I knew that they hadn't left me but they waited until I was ready for them I asked them "why have you given me this pain this is the worst ever" I was told "it was her time she is here with you now and will never leave you." then I heard her voice that I had been longing to hear she whispered "mum I love you" I came out of my deep meditated state and found that I had been crying my cheeks and eyes were wet with the tears but I felt calmer and more at peace.

I started to notice the sun shining and felt more at peace and then I had an urge to do the workshops again and also to work on the website I had neglected everyone and everything, I found that I wanted to do things again.

I found myself smiling when I was thinking of Katie and I was not crying as often, life was beginning again after all it had lain dormant for so long.

Katie was making herself known too around the house we often had a smell of her perfume wafting around the house and we even had lights flickering also things had been moved about too.

Steve did not believe this, until one particular day he was watching his favourite programme that he and Katie both enjoyed watching together. All of a sudden he had a very strong smell of perfume next to him and he said to me "god your perfume is strong today" I replied that "I hadn't any on" and he leant over to have a sniff of my neck and said "you haven't have you?

"So where is the smell coming from"? I looked at him and said "its Katie's perfume" with that he didn't believe me and said "stop talking stupid"! So with that remark I stood up and said "ok come with me" I walked out and went to the spare room picked out her perfume from the treasure chest that I had put Katie's belongings in, gave it to him and said "is that the smell"?

He sniffed the bottle I had handed to him and said "yes it is" then it dawned on him his eyes started to fill with tears he said "Christ she is here isn't she"?

I hugged him and said "yes she is she used to enjoy watching that programme with you she is letting you know she is with you again". He said "oh Christ I believe you now".

Later that night I thanked my angels for being there and helping me I also said good night to Katie and said "just give me and Steve a sign that you are here".

As we were dropping off to sleep that night both Steve and I felt something sit on the end of the bed he sat up at the same time as me thinking the dog had jumped on the bed but the dog was no where to be seen nothing was at the end of the bed.

He turned and said you felt it too? I said drowsily yes I did then I secretly thanked Katie and in my mind I said to her "I know you are with us now I will always love you".

Then Steve and I snuggled back down under the duvet and he said "bet it was Katie" I just smiled and whispered "yes it is" and for the first time in many months I slept through the night.

Katie now helps me when I do my healing and she helps me with readings and has made herself known to her sister who is now showing signs of psychic abilities it is as if Katie wants to help her and guide her too, Claire-Louise is now embracing it and not being afraid of what she can see. So with my help and Katie she is learning to use this ability.

The sun is shining again and we are all embracing life looking to the future again with trepidation wondering what will come around the corner but with renewed energy and vitality and love for one another we shall overcome those obstacles.

Even though Katie is not with me in life, but as she always said she would never leave us, in death she will never leave our side either.

.... The daughter never ever gives up on the mother, just as the mother never gives up on the daughter.

There is a tie here so strong that nothing can break it. I called it "the unbreakable bond".

Rachel Billington, b1942,

From the "Sunday Times" March 13 1994

I have started to relish my spiritual work and my dearest wish is to show and teach others how to use their abilities to connect with their angels.

So as my life goes on with twists and turns I still have many crossroads to cross and I am meeting new friends, memories and experiences along the way. I have learned that I have a genuine love for all kinds of people I love to see them progress and I get a buzz when I see their confidence soar! I have learned that I love what I do and learned that balance in life is vital for your wellbeing and health, letting go is a challenge but holding pain is very painful if you learn to forgive yourself then the pressure of keeping things bitter diminishes. I have accepted and learned that difficulties are a challenge, an opportunity to progress and learn from the mistakes

I have made. I will probably still continue to make mistakes but that is another book to write!

I still firmly believe that my soul has still not learned its life lessons I will only know when I have learned them all is when my children and family also my beloved Angels come to take me home.

Acknowledgments

First I would like to thank my darling husband Steve for believing and standing by my side through thick and thin love you forever

I would also like to thank my daughter Claire who encouraged me to carry on when I was struggling to find the words.

As a result of my mothers attitude I have learned many things and one of them was determination!

My good friend Julie who has been my best friend for over twenty years we have been through a lot together and continue to do so,

And also my new friends, Angie who has helped create my website and sorts me out when I do things wrong. What would I do with out you!

Phoenix is my dog who has sat beside through my tears and smiles while I wrote this book.

My friend penny that brought Katie to me when I needed her she was my life line. And last but not least my beautiful daughter Katie who is always by my side now in spirit.

ANGEL BLESSINGS to you all
Thank you

My beautiful girls
Claire-Louise, Kayleigh, Katie.